"I would pay 10 or 110 times the cover price for just the table of contents of this extraordinary book. In fact, I suggest you post the contents page on your work or home office wall and use it as an all-you-need-to-know daily checklist/spur to action. Please, please do not 'read' *A New Way to Think*. Ingest it, immerse yourself in it—head and, especially, heart. It is spot-on and, if applied assiduously, I guarantee it will change your life, the lives of those you work with, and the community in which you work."

—**TOM PETERS,** management guru; bestselling author,
In Search of Excellence

"Roger Martin has an undeniable gift for simplifying the complex and nuanced scenarios of management and strategy down to the main thing. And the main thing is not always what you assume it is. Often, we get in our own way when solving problems with a new way of thinking, because we're afraid it won't yield better results than the tried-and-true methods of yesterday. Martin gives us a framework for thinking through the most common problems with a new lens on what might work to bring about the most effective, long-term solution."

—**JULIA HARTZ,** cofounder and CEO, Eventbrite

"*A New Way to Think* is an essential how-to guide for building organizations that thrive—through today's uncertainties and long into the future. Like a day with a great mentor, this book burns through trendy management pablum to give readers the hidden truths and timeless questions their organization really needs to reach its potential."

—**ZACHARY FIRST,** Executive Director, Drucker Institute

"In *A New Way to Think*, Roger Martin unpacks why so many cherished frameworks in business aren't working and gives us smarter alternatives."

—**DREW HOUSTON,** CEO, Dropbox

"Rather than replacing traditional models with better models, I favor Roger Martin's underlying proposition in this book, which is to replace traditional ways of thinking with new ways of thinking. New ways of thinking must shift from centering around the organization to centering around human value."

—**ZHANG RUIMIN,** founder and Chairman, Emeritus, Board of Directors, Haier Group

"Waze for executive leadership. Through succinct and entertaining vignettes, Roger Martin helps you navigate the terrain, make the right choices, and avoid falling victim to common mistakes. *A New Way to Think* is an important read for anyone leading an organization!"

—**STEPHANIE COHEN,** Global Cohead, Consumer and Wealth Management, Goldman Sachs

"In order to stay nimble and competitive, you need to challenge your most basic assumptions on the best way to do business. No one does this more insightfully than Roger Martin. Read *A New Way to Think* to help you face your toughest decisions and to survive and thrive as a leader."

—**ALEX OSTERWALDER,** cofounder, Strategyzer; bestselling coauthor, *Business Model Generation*

A New Way
to Think

A New Way to Think

to Think

Your Guide to Superior
Management Effectiveness

Roger L. Martin

Harvard Business Review Press

Boston, Massachusetts

The web addresses referenced in this book were live and correct at the time of the book's publication but may be subject to change.

Library of Congress Cataloging-in-Publication Data

Names: Martin, Roger L., author.
Title: A new way to think : your guide to superior management effectiveness /
    Roger L. Martin.
Description: Boston, Massachusetts : Harvard Business Review Press, [2022] |
    Includes index.
Identifiers: LCCN 2021059746 (print) | LCCN 2021059747 (ebook) |
    ISBN 9781647823511 (hardcover) | ISBN 9781647823528 (epub)
Subjects: LCSH: Creative ability in business. | Success in business. |
    Industrial management. | Organizational effectiveness.
Classification: LCC HD53 .M36444 2022 (print) | LCC HD53 (ebook) |
    DDC 650.1—dc23/eng/20220107
LC record available at https://lccn.loc.gov/2021059746
LC ebook record available at https://lccn.loc.gov/2021059747

Cataloging-in-Publication data is forthcoming.

ISBN: 978-1-64782-351-1
eISBN: 978-1-64782-352-8

The paper used in this publication meets the requirements of the American National Standard for Permanence of Paper for Publications and Documents in Libraries and Archives Z39.48-1992.

To Marie-Louise, the love of my life

Contents

A New Way
to Think

Thinking Differently about the Essentials of Management

t's often said that insanity is doing the same thing over and over again but expecting different results. By that definition, I have seen plenty of it in my four decades as a strategy adviser.

When executives and managers find that a given framework, general practice, theory, or way of thinking—what I will call a "model" for short—doesn't lead to the desired outcome, they almost automatically assume that the model in question wasn't applied rigorously enough. The prescription, therefore, is to apply the model again, more vigorously. And when that produces the same unsatisfactory result, the prescription is to try even harder. If focusing on maximizing shareholder value doesn't maximize shareholder value, then focus more singularly on shareholder value. If making execution a priority doesn't result in better execution, make execution still more of a priority. If your culture doesn't change in the direction you want, then mandate culture change even more aggressively.

Existing models are extraordinarily persistent in the face of ineffectiveness and that is because our use of models to organize our thinking and action is so automatic. As MIT Sloan system dynamics professor John Sterman points out, human beings don't consciously make a choice of whether to model; "it is only a question of which model." On that "which" front, we prefer to apply a known and accepted way of thinking about a problem at hand because we know that thinking from first principles, as we sometimes must do when we encounter an unprecedented situation for which we have no model, is arduous, time-consuming, and downright scary. And once we have been confronted by that novel situation, next time round we'll almost certainly apply some form of the model we eventually figured out. We favor using existing available models because it's easier and quicker. This inclination is reinforced over and over in our formal training. From the very start, the education system teaches us models—how to multiply, how to structure a paragraph, how to categorize species— and gets us to practice using them over and over until each becomes second nature.

Business education is no different. It teaches a vast array of models— Five Forces, CAPM, the 4 Ps, EOQ, Black Scholes, GAAP, WACC, to name just a few. Over time, competing models battle for dominance, and as happens in nature with species, there is typically convergence on a dominant design in each domain in management. The winners tend to become received business wisdom. These winners get used over and over again, becoming the default framework in the contexts for which they were designed. It should come as no surprise, therefore, that when one of these models doesn't seem to work, the manager in question won't reject the model but will instead assume personal responsibility for failing to correctly apply it. It's extremely difficult—and socially risky—to question an established model that many people believe and to start building a new model from scratch.

That questioning and building has become my job, though it took me a while through the process of working with my clients to figure that it indeed was my job. Executives, mainly CEOs, hire me to help them improve the performance of their companies. That usually means that there is something that frustrates or worries them in some way— something that isn't working as well as they wish, or they wouldn't have hired me in the first place. To help them, I need to diagnose why the results aren't what they wish. It has become clear to me over the years that in nearly every case, the poor results weren't down to their not working diligently enough in pursuit of their goals; it was because the model that guided their actions wasn't up to the task.

In one classic example, a client hired me to figure out why its R&D program was producing smaller and smaller wins even though the company had invested ever more time and energy in screening R&D projects through a rigorous gating procedure that weeded out the projects that showed less promise. Despite all that rigor, the company hadn't had a real breakthrough product in several years. What quickly became clear to me is that the model implicitly guiding its actions was that early screening based on the rigorous analysis of available market data would increase R&D productivity through eliminating unlikely prospects, thereby freeing up time and resources for the more promising prospects.

On the surface, that model made sense. But when I looked closely at the process, I realized that the screening methodology the client used involved projecting future sales based on currently existing data. This meant that for innovations that were minor variations on the status quo, relatively compelling data tended to be available, and these projects consistently made it through the various gates. For more breakthrough innovations, however, there just wasn't good data available (because the ideas were new), and hence, projections of huge future sales tended to be dismissed as speculative. In other words, the seemingly sensible model was logically flawed: it was predicated on the availability of good market data, but existing market data is not likely to be relevant for genuinely breakthrough innovations.

So was there a different model the company could use instead? There was and it is based on American pragmatist philosopher Charles Sanders Peirce's observation that no new idea in the history of the world has been proven in advance analytically, which means that if you insist on rigorous proof of the merits of an idea during its development, you will kill it if it is truly a breakthrough idea, because there will be no proof of its breakthrough characteristics in advance. If you are going to screen innovation projects, therefore, a better model is one that has you assess them on the strength of their logic—the theory of why the idea is a good one—not on the strength of the existing data. Then, as you get further into each project that passes the logic test, you need to look for ways to create data that enables you to test and adjust—or perhaps kill—the idea as you develop it.

In the case of my client with the R&D problem—and thousands of others like it—applying the model more diligently wasn't the answer. Solving the problem required *a new way to think*. It required a different model. That became the heart of my work. Rather than accept a client's existing model, I would step back to ask what it was about the model that caused it to fail to meet the needs of the problem it was designed to address. And, more importantly, was there a different, more powerful way to think about the problem?

Looking back over my career now, I realize that I have always been fascinated by models because of the degree to which they shape everything we do. From elementary school onward throughout my formal education, I probed the models that my teachers and professors taught me. How did they know that the world worked that way? Were they sure? Did it work in all cases? Asking these questions was how I learned and how I got to what I thought was a better answer. And while I am sure that a lot of my teachers, bosses, and clients have found my constant questioning annoying, a fair few have also found the questions interesting and have acted on the answers we came up with together. And that brings me to this book.

Models, *Harvard Business Review,* and a Book

Whenever I find that one of my alternative models is helpful across multiple clients for addressing a given class of problems, I write about it to share the advice more widely. My favorite place to do so has been *Harvard Business Review* (HBR) with my favorite editorial partner, senior editor David Champion, with whom I have written twenty HBR articles since our first piece together in 2010.

Not all the articles with David take on a dominant model that is not producing the outcomes desired and provide a superior alternative. But at one point during our collaborations, David noted that a goodly number of them did, and broached the idea of doing a whole book in that vein. This book is the fruit of that conversation. Each of the fourteen self-contained chapters compares a dominant but flawed model to an alternative that I argue is superior.

I am, however, not so arrogant to claim my alternative is the right model or a perfect model. I come from the Karl Popper/Imre Lakatos school of falsificationism. Like them, I don't believe there are right answers or wrong answers, just better ones and worse ones. One should always use the best model available, but watch closely to see whether it produces the outcomes that it promised. If it does, keep using it. If it doesn't, then you should work on creating a better model— one that produces results more in keeping with your goals. But be assured that in due course your new model, too, will be found wanting and will be replaced by a better model still.

I'm aware that many managers and executives are trained as scientists, and when you've been trained that way, you may well think that there is, indeed, a right answer or model to apply in any given situation. If that's what you think, though, I should remind you that Sir Isaac Newton's models of physics were widely taught as absolutely right for over a century, until such time that the world figured out, thanks to Albert Einstein, that they weren't exactly right but just mainly right. I'm not promising to provide fourteen correct models in this book. I'm proposing, rather, that my fourteen new or different models will provide a better likelihood of getting you an outcome you want than the model it replaces. And I would welcome the next thinker who will improve on each of my models.

Finally, I want to point out that across the fourteen chapters, you will find that I make disproportionate use of Procter & Gamble (P&G) as an example and frequently mention its former CEO A.G. Lafley. The reason for this is that I have had a uniquely long and productive relationship with P&G, having worked nearly continuously as an adviser to the company since 1986. I have had the pleasure advising a number of P&G CEOs in that time, from the late John Smale in the late 1980s to the just-retired David Taylor, but my longest and deepest single relationship was with A.G. Lafley, who served as CEO for thirteen years across two stints. We were thinking partners to the extent that two of the fourteen chapters are based on HBR articles that we coauthored, and, of course, we coauthored the book *Playing to Win*.

As a consequence of that long and deep relationship with P&G, I had an up-close vantage point on many situations on which I worked, and which provide great illustrations of the concepts in the book. Because I know the circumstances and facts of these cases, I would rather use them than second- or thirdhand stories. On top of which, P&G also has the advantage of being an extremely well-known consumer products company to which readers will perhaps more readily relate than they might to an industrial services company that they may never have heard of. But I am very well aware that many other companies equally illustrate what is meritorious in business as does P&G.

By design, the fourteen chapters in this book don't build on one another in a way that absolutely requires them to be read in order. They can be read in order of interest or left to read until the situation described in the chapter arises. In that sense, you can treat this as a management handbook. That said, I am an academic and a consultant, and both professions have a strong interest in categorizing ideas, and as I was putting the chapters together, I mentally grouped them into four general buckets, which helped me to figure out the order I wanted to present them in. So here goes . . .

On Context

My first bucket deals with context or, maybe, the framework in which most corporations operate. Three topics seemed to me to belong to this group and are discussed in part 1:

1. Competition. The classic model holds that corporations compete, and a central job of the corporate level is to organize and control the levels below it. A more effective model holds that competition happens at the front line where real customers are served, and that the job of every corporate level above the frontline level is to help the level below it to serve that customer better.

2. Stakeholders. Even though under pressure now, the dominant model in practice still holds that the corporation exists to serve the shareholders and therefore shareholders come first in priority. A more effective model holds that putting shareholders first is a bad way to enrich shareholders. Rather, putting customers first is what will lead to the success of the corporation—and the enrichment of shareholders.

3. Customers. The dominant model is that the corporation should focus on customer loyalty as the key driver of its success. A more effective model holds that unconscious habit is a much more powerful driver of the customer behavior that a corporation should pursue than is conscious loyalty.

Making Choices

My next bucket focuses on how managers within a corporation make decisions. Two topics seemed to belong in this bucket: deal with the act of making choices within the corporation, discussed in part 2:

4. Strategy. The traditional model in strategy is to focus on asking the question: What is true? A more effective model for framing and making strategy choices is to focus on the logic behind the choice by asking: What would have to be true?

5. Data. The traditional model holds that in order to be rigorous, one must insist on making data-based decisions. A more effective model holds that in one domain of the world, that is correct, but in another it leads to dangerously flawed choices, and there, imagination is critical.

Structuring Work

Having made their key choices, managers have to figure out how to deliver on those choices, so my next bucket is about structuring work, discussed in part 3. Three topics seemed to belong here:

6. Culture. The dominant model is that culture is so centrally important that if it is not conducive to the working of the

corporation, those in charge must change culture by mandating a change and/or reorganizing to produce the desired culture change. A more effective model is to hold that culture can't be changed by mandating it or formally reorganizing roles and responsibilities. Rather it can only be changed indirectly by altering how individuals work with each other.

7. **Knowledge work.** The dominant model is to organize knowledge work the way we organize physical work—on the basis of full-time jobs that are assumed to be permanently involved in performing the same set of activities. A more effective model is to organize knowledge work and workers around time-bound projects.

8. **Corporate functions.** The dominant model is that corporate functions are there to faithfully execute the strategies of the operating businesses, which are the only units in the corporation that should have strategies. A more effective model is that corporate functions need strategies to be effective to the same extent that operating businesses do.

Key Activities

Having structured how people work, I went deeper into a number of key activities in which most units in a given business engage. This category makes up the six remaining chapters of the book, in part 4:

9. **Planning.** The dominant model makes business planning equivalent to strategy-making. The trouble with this is that planning is more about managing risks and becoming comfortable with them than about assuming them. A more effective model distinguishes strategy development as a process of

choosing goals and risks rather than one in which you seek to control risks on your path toward a goal you haven't really examined.

10. Execution. The dominant model holds that first you formulate or choose your strategy and then you execute or implement it. A more effective model sees no dividing line between "strategy" and "execution." Rather, both are identically making choices under uncertainty, constraints, and competition.

11. Talent. The dominant model holds that compensation, especially performance-based incentive compensation, is the most critical element in attracting and retaining high-end talent. A more effective model sees treating each talented employee as an individual with unique needs and desires as the key to attraction and retention.

12. Innovation. The dominant model holds that the focus of attention and investment should be on creating the innovative artifact, whether product, service, business model, and so on. A more effective model sees that the design of the intervention that enables the innovation to be approved and successfully launched is of equal importance as the design of the artifact itself.

13. Capital investment. The dominant model of accounting for capital investments is to place them on the balance sheet at cost (less accumulated depreciation), calculate profitability based on that as denominator, and make decisions based on profitability thus calculated. A more effective model treats that asset as what it is worth immediately after being converted from unfettered capital to embedded capital and calculates returns based on that embedded value.

14. M&A. The dominant model of M&A is that a corporation makes an acquisition primarily to gain an attractive asset or capability from the acquired entity. A more effective model holds that a key goal in any acquisition should be to provide more value to the acquired entity than the corporation receives from the entity.

The fourteen dominant models are in place not because they are stupid. All of them make a lot of sense. So, I don't believe that these one-sentence descriptions of the alternative models will convince you to jettison the dominant model and adopt my alternative suggestion. But my hope is that you will be intrigued enough to read the whole chapter for each and will be convinced to at least experiment with using the alternative model. If you do, I am confident you will become a still more effective executive, and, like my hero Peter Drucker, my primary writing goal is just that: to help executives increase their effectiveness.

On Context

Competition

It happens at the front line,
not at the head office.

I n the popular narrative, business competition takes place between
companies: Boeing vs. Airbus; General Motors vs. Toyota vs. Volks-
wagen; Microsoft vs. Amazon vs. Google; Procter & Gamble vs.
L'Oréal vs. Unilever vs. Johnson & Johnson; or Coca-Cola vs. Pepsi-
Co. It's tempting to think of these great companies as colonizing
nations engaged in a world war, fighting for territory and position in
multiple theaters of combat, and it's quite likely that many CEOs agree,
to judge from the emphasis in the press on a company's market share.

But it's not corporations that compete—it's the products and services they provide. Customers of narrow-body commercial jets think
that the B737 competes with the A320. Buyers of midsize sedans think
Malibu competes with Camry, which competes with Passat. Customers of cloud services think Azure competes with AWS, which
competes with Google Cloud. Shampoo buyers think Pantene competes with Fructis, which competes with Dove, which competes with

Neutrogena. And beverages? Well, if it is diet colas, it is Diet Coke vs. Diet Pepsi. If it is orange juice, it is Minute Maid vs. Tropicana. If it is sports drinks, it is Powerade vs. Gatorade. And if it is bottled water, it is Dasani vs. Aquafina.

And that brings us to a better way of thinking about competition: *it happens at the front line more so than at the head office.* Individual customers choose between products and services that hold the potential for meeting their needs. And these customers have only a limited amount of visibility into or concern with who actually brings the product or service at their front line, let alone the layers between the product on the shelf and where and by whom it is made and delivered. A poor product or service at the front line won't be saved in the eyes of customers by being part of a particular corporation, even if that corporation has other related products that are successful. Take Microsoft Windows. Even though many Mac users like Microsoft's Office suite, it doesn't convert them to Windows.

Understanding competition as something that happens around individual customers at the front line rather than as a war between organizations upends much of what managers assume, consciously or not, about mission, strategy, culture, organization, and decision-making. As I'll argue in the following pages, leading businesses needs to be seen less as a challenge of managing organizational complexity and more about making sure that value is maximized at the front lines. This calls for an approach that is less inspired by hierarchy and more by respect for the insights of the people in direct contact with customers, structured and motivated not around optimizing the use of their existing resources and capabilities but rather around identifying what's needed to deliver value right in front of the customer. In this environment, leadership must be focused squarely on figuring out how the organization can mobilize its assets and resources to deliver the biggest bang at the front line.

From Optimal Hierarchy . . .

Although a product competes on the front line, what goes into making it competitive obviously does not happen there; corporations must bring together many resources and capabilities to create new products. Consequently, firms become complex organizations.

The traditional response to complex organizational challenges is to create hierarchy, an organizational model in which experienced, wise leaders inform themselves of the facts on the ground, reflect and consult, and then give orders to people below them, which inform the orders that those people give to people below them and so on. That's why in every corporation, we see numerous levels above the front line. If the front line is Pantene shampoo, above Pantene is the Hair Care business, and above that is Beauty Care, and above that is Procter & Gamble.

Of course, there's considerable variation around how hierarchy works across different national cultures, but one way or another, in most countries the assumption is that success in hierarchical organizations has traditionally been largely determined by the quality of the judgments cascading down from the people at the top because, so the logic goes, the people at the top have the best view of how the battle is going overall and where they should send their troops and with what weapons.

But in business, where competition is between products rather than companies, the line of sight between a CEO's decisions and whether a customer will buy a product at any given time is much less clear. The individual outcomes of customers' decisions are far from easy for executives, removed from the front line, to predict and control. This changes the power dynamics inside the corporation—who determines what is and isn't valuable and how the rest of the organization relates to the businesses directly engaged with the company's products and services.

. . . to Organizing for Value

If the judge of the value of any product or service is the customer who chooses to buy, not the provider, then it is the provider's people at the front line, in front of the customer, who are best placed to determine what the customer values. It is up to the rest of the company to help the people in the front lines, where the revenues come in, to satisfy those customer needs. The lower level, in effect, is the customer of the level above it. And like a customer, it should expect to get more value from those services than it pays to get them. Hair Care needs to add net competitive value to Pantene, whether by doing scale-effective hair care R&D across the six major hair care brands globally or in some other way.

The same rule applies to each subsequent level of aggregation. Just as Hair Care level needs to add more value to Pantene than it costs Pantene at the front line, Beauty Care has to help Hair Care in its goal of creating more value for Pantene than it costs Pantene. Perhaps it can add value by developing proprietary understanding of beauty customers across its $13 billion beauty business that would be hard for Hair Care to develop on its own. And P&G has to help Beauty Care to help Hair Care to help Pantene. P&G can do that by making it cheaper for Beauty Care to buy advertising for Hair Care, in general, and Pantene, specifically, thanks to P&G's huge advertising scale.

In every case, if a layer is not generating net value that ultimately helps the product win at the front line, then that layer is at best superfluous and worst makes the product less competitive. If P&G's Beauty Care division can't help the Hair Care help Pantene more than it costs Hair Care to support it, then P&G should consider whether to elimi-

These are only examples of utilizing operating scale and cumulative investment to provide a service to the front line at a lower cost than it would cost at the front line alone. There are many others, including hiring, training and development, government relations, or regulatory compliance. But whatever type of value is added at each layer, it needs to exceed the inevitable costs that the layer imposes.

This poses two challenges. First of all, managers in the layer above have got to start treating the people below them as customers—understanding their lives and needs, stepping into their shoes. That sounds obvious, but it is surprising how remote executives become as you go up the hierarchy. For example, I worked with a major auto OEM in the mid-2000s and came to realize that every six months, each senior executive automatically had a brand-new vehicle delivered to the executive parking garage below their offices. Every day when they arrived with their car, it was cleaned, serviced, and if necessary, refueled. As a consequence, they had lost touch with what customers experienced when buying, financing, servicing, and operating their vehicles. This mindset has to change, and the change has to start from the top. How can you expect managers in the middle layers to treat those below them as customers if you don't pay them the compliment yourself? To remedy, I had each executive, including the CEO, do in-home visits with both their own and competitor customers to familiarize themselves with life at the front line.

Smart CEOs do this instinctively. During his entire time as CEO, A.G. Lafley had a rule that whenever he visited another country, he needed the local P&G organization to set up an in-home visit with a local consumer and a store walk-through at a local retailer. His visit to the bank of a river in rural western China to speak to the village women who washed their clothes there became legendary. The message was clear: If the global CEO isn't too busy to do in-home visits and store checks, how is it that you are?

Once they've ensured that managers at all levels have gotten a good understanding of their customers and what those customers need, corporate executives can start on the second challenge.

Creating a Theory for the Firm

How can the corporation add net value to all businesses in the next level of the portfolio—and how does it ensure that all businesses in that next level are capable of adding value to the subsequent level, and so on? Specifically, how does P&G make sure it adds net value to Laundry & Home Care, Baby & Feminine Care, Beauty, Grooming, Health Care, and Family Care? How does PepsiCo make sure it adds net value to Frito-Lay, Quaker Foods, and PepsiCo Beverages? How does Microsoft make sure it adds net value to Productivity & Business Processes, Intelligent Cloud, and Other Personal Computing?

Answering these questions requires thinking about both what capabilities and resources to acquire and what parts of the business really belong together. This is a classic chicken-and-egg dilemma. You can't build value-adding capabilities until you know the portfolio members for whom you are building said value. But you can't know what portfolio members you should have until you know that it is possible to add net value to each. This means that corporate leaders need to iterate back and forth to home in on the combination of portfolio composition and value-adding rationale(s). Let's look at what that involves.

Because each diversified corporation already has a portfolio, the status quo is the practical place to start. The corporate level needs to develop a draft value-adding rationale for the next level. It is just like classic business unit or product strategy, in which the heart of strategy is composed of the linked where-to-play and how-to-win questions. In this case, the former question should focus on choosing in which capability domains to invest, and the latter question on choosing in what way to utilize corporate scale or cumulative investment in the chosen capabilities to make the next level net better off. With a draft value-adding rationale for the next level in place, management in each part of that level should ask the same set of questions about its draft value-adding rationale for each business in the next level. And then the next level and the next, until you get to the level directly above the front line.

This first iteration of corporate strategy from top to bottom should produce four intermediate outputs for refining in the next round. Typically, it takes two or three rounds of back-and-forth to achieve coherence across the portfolio. The four intermediate outputs are the following.

The key capabilities needed to serve customers at the front line

Begin by identifying what capabilities to invest in and at what level you should invest in them in order to support what improvements or enhancements to which businesses at the front line. Should you invest in creating a shared distribution capability at the business group level that would support multiple businesses across multiple products? Or should you invest in a shared R&D center that would support multiple products across one business? And what would these capabilities and resources cost?

A.G. Lafley carried out this exercise shortly after becoming CEO of P&G in mid-2000. In early 2001, he convened an offsite with his global leadership team to determine what the key capabilities then underpinning the P&G portfolio were—what they came to call the "reinforcing rods." Literally over one hundred were posited and were winnowed down to three, which were expanded to five over time in the iterative process: (1) the ability to go-to-market (GTM) with a broad and important portfolio of products delivered by way of multifunctional, customer-colocated teams (like the P&G Walmart team in Bentonville, Arkansas; (2) the capability to create compelling and meaningful innovations for consumers; (3) deep consumer understanding that provides proprietary insights; (4) the ability to build trusted and compelling brands; and (5) the scale to accomplish all of the above at an effective cost.

The customers, products, and services you should drop

If there are businesses at the front line that can't be helped by being part of the organization, they should be removed from the portfolio before the cost to their ability to compete at the front line is reflected in diminishing competitiveness and profitability. Since costs are inevitable and benefits are not, figuring this out sooner rather than later is in the interest of both the corporation and the business in question, though the process of cleaning house can turn into a long-term project.

At P&G, the identification of the key corporate reinforcing rods triggered a fifteen-year process of finding better homes for businesses that corporate could not help enough to cover the costs to those businesses of being owning by P&G. It was a huge effort that involved numerous multibillion-dollar sales. The food businesses (Jif peanut butter, Crisco oils, Pringles potato chips, and Folgers coffee) were sold because of the limited ability to continuously innovate to produce advantage, even though most were market leaders in their category. The pharmaceutical, pet care, and professional salon businesses were sold largely because their specialized GTM was so different from the food, drug, and mass merchandiser channels in which P&G had expertise and leverage. The beauty businesses that featured the weakest role for technological innovation like color cosmetics, fine fragrances, and hair colorants were sold. Over a hundred smaller brands across the portfolio were sold because, at their modest scale, P&G could not bring to bear its capabilities in innovation and brand building. And by 2016, the remaining seventy brands with attractive scale were clustered in ten remaining categories (from a maximum of over twenty) in which P&G could bring all five of the key capabilities to bear.

The customers, products, and services you should add

If the corporation can bring to bear substantial advantages to either an existing portfolio business or a business not currently in the portfolio, either of these should be taken as a signal for investing to expand the portfolio in that direction. So even as P&G engaged in a monumental paring exercise, which included approximately $30 billion in divestitures, it bulked up in areas in which it could apply the advantages from the key capabilities. It bought Clairol to bulk up its already successful hair care business. It bought the Merck consumer health business to strengthen its personal health care business. Unlike the divested pharmaceutical business, which required a specialized sales force for a channel unique for P&G (the physician and hospital channel), the consumer health business fit perfectly within P&G's core GTM. With the acquisition of Gillette, P&G entered grooming, a new category that benefited from all of P&G's key capabilities. Plus, as a bonus Gillette's Oral-B oral care business fit perfectly with and bulked up P&G's existing oral care business (Crest and Scope).

The layers you should eliminate

As noted earlier, if any layer in the company is incapable of adding net value to the businesses below it, the level should be eliminated because it is hurting competitiveness at the front line, whether that is observable yet or not. Note this should not be symmetric. If business group A is not adding value to the businesses below it, that fact does not imply that other business groups B and C that are serving other frontline businesses below them should be disbanded—just the offender A that is not adding value to its frontline businesses.

At P&G, this trimming happened with the geographic level of region presidents. Since a major reorganization in 1998, six regional presidents (e.g., North America or Western Europe) coordinated the GTM activities across all categories in their region. But that coordination had a cost, both in terms of the regional president organizations, which were not small, and in the time and effort it took for the global category presidents to accomplish their goals for the region in conjunction with the customer teams in that region. So, in 2019, for the top ten countries accounting for 80 percent of P&G sales and 90 percent of profits, the level was eliminated, and the global category presidents were directly responsible for GTM. (The numerous remaining smaller countries were grouped under one executive responsible for working with the line of global category presidents in a manner like the regional presidents had done before.)

The process outlined here requires a lot of work. It doesn't take much size and diversification to get pretty complicated, pretty quickly. Imagine a modestly diversified corporation with two business groups, each of which has two businesses, each of which has two distinct product categories. That means the need for strategy choices that create net value-added for fourteen different internal customers (two business groups plus four businesses plus eight product categories). If it is flatter but a bit broader, with one fewer level and featuring corporate, three businesses, and three product categories each, it is still twelve different internal customers. And it gets rapidly more complex from there.

• • •

Because most companies don't build corporate strategy from the perspective of increasing the competitiveness at their front line, their corporate structures tend to swell rapidly in terms of both costs and decision-making. As a consequence, the dominant motif is cost reduction, delayering, and decentralization by pushing decision-making closer to the front line. And if the company doesn't do these things on its own, there are activist hedge funds lurking to force that exact program on them. To be sure, this delayering may be better than just leaving the organization as it is. But to reduce a company's strategy to the elimination of corporate bloat means that you are leaving on the table all the value that creativity, energy, and imagination can produce. Proactively structuring corporate strategy from the front line back is what will create opportunities for your businesses at the front line, not for your competitors.

2

Stakeholders

To actually create shareholder value,
put customers before shareholders.

odern capitalism can be broken down into two major eras.
The first, managerial capitalism, began in 1932 and was
defined by the then-radical notion that firms ought to have
professional management. The second, shareholder value capitalism,
began in 1976. Its governing premise is that the purpose of every corporation should be to maximize shareholder wealth. If firms pursue this
goal, the thinking goes, both shareholders and society will benefit.

Both eras were heralded by an influential academic work. In 1932,
Adolf A. Berle and Gardiner C. Means published their legendary trea-
tise, *The Modern Corporation and Private Property*, which asserted
that management should be divorced from ownership. After that, the
business world would no longer be dominated by CEO owners like
the Rockefellers, Mellons, Carnegies, and Morgans. Firms would be
run by the hired help, a new class of professional CEO. This movement, said Berle and Means, was not to be feared; it was part of a brave
new era of economic expansion (which would actually take a few years
to get going, as it turned out, owing to the Great Depression).

The idea caught on. While there certainly continued to be owner-CEOs, professional managers came to dominate the corner office. Entrepreneurs were welcome to start up new firms but would be wise to hand them over to professional managers, who were more dependable and less volatile once the business reached a significant size.

Then in 1976 managerial capitalism received a stinging rebuke: Michael C. Jensen and William H. Meckling's "Theory of the Firm: Managerial Behavior, Agency Costs and Ownership Structure," published in the *Journal of Financial Economics*. The paper, which has gone on to become the most-cited academic business article of all time, argued that owners were getting short shrift from professional managers, who enhanced their own financial well-being rather than that of the shareholders. This was bad for shareholders and wasteful for the economy, Jensen and Meckling argued; the managers were squandering corporate and societal resources to feather their own nests.

Their critique ushered in a new philosophy of capitalism, as CEOs quickly saw the need to swear allegiance to "maximizing shareholder value." Boards of directors soon came to view their job as aligning the interests of senior management with those of shareholders through the use of stock-based compensation. No longer would the shareholder be abused—the shareholder would be king.

But have shareholders become significantly better off since they displaced managers as the center of the business universe? Not really. From 1933 to the end of 1976, when they were allegedly playing second fiddle to professional managers, S&P 500 shareholders earned compound annual real returns of 7.6 percent. From 1977 to 2020, they've been an eerily similar 7.8 percent. On this basis, it's hard to argue that much has changed for shareholders as a result of this supposedly radical shake-up.

That finding begs a more provocative follow-up: If the shareholders were all you cared about, would focusing on increasing shareholder value necessarily be the best way to make sure they benefited? Which brings us to a different way of thinking about who you should make your primary stakeholder: *To actually create shareholder value, put your customers before your shareholders.* In other words—and nobody should be surprised by this—Peter Drucker had it right when he said that the primary purpose of a business is to acquire and keep customers. As this chapter will demonstrate, a single-minded focus on profits guarantees you won't get them.

I'll begin by looking at the problems with putting shareholders first.

The Flawed Logic of Shareholder Value

While the concept of shareholder value maximization has always been attractive in its elegance, making it a reality has proved tricky for managers. This difficulty is unavoidable because of the way shareholder value is created.

Shareholders have a residual claim on a firm's assets and earnings, meaning they get what's left after all other claimants—employees and their pension funds, suppliers, tax-collecting governments, debt holders, and preferred shareholders (if any exist)—are paid. The value of their shares, therefore, is the discounted value of all future cash flows minus those payments. Since the future is unknowable, potential shareholders must estimate what that cash flow will be; their collective expectations about the future determine the stock price. Any shareholders who expect that the discounted value of future equity earnings of the company will be less than the current price will sell their stock. Any potential shareholders who expect that the discounted future value will exceed the current price will buy stock.

This means that shareholder value has almost nothing to do with the present. Indeed, present earnings tend to be a small fraction of the value of common shares. Over the past decade, the average yearly price-earnings multiple for the S&P 500 has been 22x, meaning that current earnings represent less than 5 percent of stock prices.

Undoubtedly, if expectations for a company's future performance are optimistic, shareholder value will be high. In March 2021 Tesla's stock traded at a price-earnings multiple just over 135x because people believed the company's revenues and importance would continue to grow. At about the same time, the average PE ratio of other US car companies was just 16 because investors were much less optimistic about the long-term future of the traditional automakers.

For managers, the implications of this are clear: the only sure way to increase shareholder value is to raise expectations about the future performance of the company from their current level. Unfortunately, executives simply can't do that indefinitely. Shareholders will look at good results, get excited, and ratchet up their expectations to the point where managers can't continue to meet them. Indeed, it is well documented that shareholders get both overly excited about good prospects and overly despondent about bad prospects. That is why stock markets are much more volatile than the earnings of the companies in them. Over the last two decades or so, the P/E multiple of the S&P 500 has fluctuated between 123x (May 2009) and just over 5x (December 2017), and back up to 39x by the fall of 2021.

Most executives figure this out; they come to understand that shareholder value creation and destruction are cyclical and, more important, not under their control. They can push shareholder value up in short bursts, but in due course, prices will fall again. So, the executives invest in short-term strategies, hoping to get out before the inevitable crash, and often later criticize their successors for failing to avoid preordained declines. Alternatively, they manage expectations downward so that they can steadily increase shareholder value for a longer period of time. In other words, because they can't win the game they're asked to play, CEOs translate it into a game that they can and do win.

This is why the goal of shareholder value maximization and the compensation approach that goes with it are bad for shareholders. The very executives who must achieve the goal realize that they can't. Talented executives can grow market share and sales, increase margins, and use capital more efficiently, but no matter how good they are, they can't increase shareholder value if expectations get out of line with reality. The harder a CEO is pushed to increase shareholder value, the more the CEO will be tempted to make moves that actually hurt the shareholders.

Let the Customers Take Over

Determining what your customers value and focusing on always pleasing them is a better optimization formula. Of course, companies face obvious constraints on customer satisfaction; they'd quickly go bankrupt if they made customers happier by charging ever-lower prices for ever-greater value. Rather, companies should seek to maximize customer satisfaction while ensuring that shareholders earn an acceptable risk-adjusted return on their equity.

Consider Johnson & Johnson. It has the corporate world's single most eloquent statement of purpose—its "credo," which hasn't changed since J&J's legendary chair Robert Wood Johnson created it in 1943. Here it is, in abbreviated form:

> We believe our first responsibility is to the doctors, nurses, and patients, to mothers and fathers and all others who use our products and services. . . . We are responsible to our employees, the men and women who work with us throughout the world. . . . We are responsible to the communities in which we live and work and to the world community as well. . . . Our final responsibility is to our stockholders. . . . When we operate according to these principles, the stockholders should realize a fair return.

The credo bluntly spells out the pecking order: customers come first, and shareholders last. However, J&J has confidence that when customer satisfaction is at the top of the list, shareholders will do just fine.

So far, the bet has paid off. Take former CEO James Burke's handling of the 1982 Tylenol poisonings, in which seven Chicago-area consumers died after ingesting Tylenol capsules that had been tampered with. J&J's response is considered the textbook case of a company's "doing the right thing" regardless of the impact on profits. The deaths occurred only in the Chicago area, but Burke promptly issued a recall of every capsule of Tylenol across America, even though the government hadn't demanded it and Tylenol represented a fifth of J&J's profits. After the recall, sales and market share plummeted.

Commentators expressed surprise that the CEO of a publicly traded company would throw thoughts of profit to the wind and heaped praise on Burke for taking an exemplary personal moral stance. One look at the credo, however, reveals that his decision was less about his personal morals and more about J&J's clearly defined objectives. Arguably, Burke was simply following the credo as a dutiful CEO. Customers came first and stockholders came fourth—and he acted accordingly. He didn't put meeting quarterly profit expectations at the top of his list. In fact, he put it squarely at the bottom.

In the long run, that decision hasn't hurt J&J at all. In fact, loyalty toward Tylenol soared after the company demonstrated that customer safety came first and also introduced the world's first tamper-resistant packaging for over-the-counter health products. In March 2021, J&J's market capitalization stood at $418 billion, around the tenth highest in the world. J&J seems to have indeed provided long-term shareholders more than a "fair return."

Other companies have also done well by shareholders by not putting them first. P&G, the world's biggest consumer products company, which had the world's fifteenth highest market capitalization by the end of 2020, put the consumer at the center of its universe long ago. P&G's statement of purpose, values, and principles, which was written in 1986, describes a hierarchy that is strikingly similar to J&J's:

We will provide branded products and services of superior quality and value that improve the lives of the world's consumers. As a result, consumers will reward us with leadership sales, profit, and value creation, allowing our people, our shareholders and the communities in which we live and work to prosper.

Here, increased shareholder value is one of the by-products of a focus on customer satisfaction; it is clearly not the top priority.

None of this means that the companies that pioneered the pursuit of shareholder value as their central objective did badly. General Electric and Coca-Cola, for example, two of the poster children of the shareholder value movement under Jack Welch and Robert Goizueta respectively, grew shareholder value reasonably faster than the S&P 500 did during the tenure of these famous CEOs: the compound annual growth rate of GE's total shareholder return under Welch was 12.3 percent versus 10.4 percent for the S&P 500, and Coke's under Goizueta was 15 percent to the S&P 500's 10.8 percent. Even today, long after those glory days, both companies are still among the world's top 150 firms by market cap. But neither has managed to create more shareholder value over the long term than leading companies that tell shareholders in no uncertain terms to get to the back of the bus.

The Principle at Work

Why is it that companies that don't focus on maximizing shareholder value deliver such impressive returns? Because their CEOs are free to concentrate on building the real business rather than on managing shareholder expectations. When Paul Polman took over as CEO at Unilever in 2009, he delivered a tough and controversial message to shareholders. He told them that Unilever had been underinvesting in serving its consumers for the long term. It wasn't investing enough in innovating on their behalf and building their brands. He was going to put long-term innovation and branding ahead of short-term stock market considerations.

Not only that, he would make Unilever a leader in sustainability, because consumers were going to increasingly demand it. And, if shareholders didn't like his message, they should sell their stock. Many worried that the exit would crater Unilever's stock and destroy the company. It didn't. The stock traded down modestly. But the exiting shareholders were replaced by shareholders who cared about consumers long term and sustainability. Polman was widely considered to have turned around a lumbering giant and delivered a 266 percent increase in the stock price during his ten years at the helm—despite telling shareholders that they weren't his singular obsession.

Compensation is another key point of difference. When companies aren't bent on increasing shareholder value, their boards generally don't distract their CEOs with stock-based compensation that is short-term focused or realized at retirement. Short-term rewards encourage CEOs to manage short-term expectations rather than push for real progress. And rewards priced at the time of retirement only get CEOs to manage to the finish line. If, like a marathon runner, the company crashes to the ground after crossing it, that's someone else's problem. One has only to look at a historical stock chart for GE for an example. It peaked at about $60 in August 2000, a year before Welch retired with a record $417 million payoff. By the end of 2002, little more than a year after he retired, it had fallen to around $25. In 2021, it has been in the $10–$13 range as the company struggles to manage its suffocating debt load.

The structure of Lafley's compensation at P&G, by contrast, was indicative of a company with a culture of maximizing customer satisfaction. Approximately 90 percent of his total compensation was in stock options or restricted stock. While that's not highly unusual for today's CEOs, the stock options had a particularly long vesting period—three years—and a two-year subsequent holding period. Lafley also chose to hold options twice as long as required and to sell shares only under the restrictions of a planned-sale program. As for the restricted stock, which represented a significant portion of Lafley's incentive compensation, none of it actually vested before or even at retirement. The vesting period began a year after his retirement and lasted ten years. Had Lafley managed shareholders' expectations to peak at his retirement, only to fall off thereafter, he would have hurt his own compensation. Hence, for his entire tenure as CEO, he had the incentive to build the business for the very long term, groom a great successor, and leave P&G in excellent condition.

Many executives would take exception to compensation arrangements like Lafley's, arguing that they'd be unfairly exposed to the mistakes of their successors. That is where culture comes in. P&G's compensation system would indeed be unfair in a culture in which compensation is stock-based and short-term-oriented, in which it is "every man for himself." In such cultures, it is difficult to install longer-term compensation, so the culture inevitably remains "every man for himself." However, in a culture oriented toward serving the customer, a compensation structure like Lafley's makes lots of sense and isn't difficult to install—and it reinforces the behaviors that build real value for the long term. In Lafley's case, his immediate successor was a disappointment. When the board asked him, Lafley returned for another stint as CEO and several years later turned the company over to what turned out to be a highly successful CEO, David Taylor.

Even when customer value maximization is the primary objective, the culture is right, and stock-based compensation has exceedingly long vesting periods, the siren call of shareholder value maximization is ever present. At P&G, Lafley inherited a year-old compensation system that tied rewards for senior executives to total shareholder return (TSR), which was defined as the increase in share price plus dividends (if reinvested in stock) over a three-year period. Under the system, P&G's TSR was benchmarked against that of a peer group; if the company's TSR was in the upper half of the group, the executives received bonuses.

Lafley, however, quickly noticed that great TSR performance in a given year was routinely followed by poor performance the next year, because high total shareholder returns were spurred by a pronounced jump in expectations that simply couldn't be reproduced the next year. He came to realize that increases in shareholder value had very little to do with real business performance and a lot to do with the fertile imaginations of shareholders, who were speculating what the company's future might hold. This insight prompted Lafley to switch the bonus metric from TSR to something called operating TSR, which is based on a combination of three real operating performance measures—sales growth, profit margin improvement, and increase in capital efficiency. His belief was that if P&G satisfied its customers, operating TSR would increase, and the stock price would take care of itself over the long term. Moreover, operating TSR is a number that P&G's business unit presidents can truly influence, unlike the market-based TSR number.

• • •

Of course, not every company that puts customer satisfaction first will be a P&G or a J&J. But I firmly believe that if more companies made customers the top priority, the quality of corporate decision-making would improve because thinking about the customer forces you to focus on improving your operations and the products and services you provide, rather than on spinning lines to shareholders. This does not mean that you will lose cost discipline; the profit motive will not go away. Managers like profits just as much as shareholders do because the more profits the firm makes, the more money is available to pay managers. In other words, the need for a healthy share price is a natural constraint on any other objective you set. Making it the prime objective, however, creates the temptation to trade long-term gains in operations-driven value away for temporary gains in expectations-driven value. To get CEOs to focus on the first, we need to reinvent the purpose of the firm.

This chapter is adapted from Roger L. Martin, "The Age of Customer Capitalism," *Harvard Business Review*, January–February 2010.

3

Customers

The familiar solution usually trumps the perfect one.

I n May 2016 Facebook's category-leading photo-sharing application, Instagram, abandoned its original icon, a retro camera familiar to the app's 400 million plus users, and replaced it with a flat modernist design that, as the head of design explained, "suggests a camera." Under a growing threat from Instagram's rival Snapchat, he offered this rationale for the switch: The icon "was beginning to feel . . . not reflective of the community, and we thought we could make it better."

One needed only the article title to understand the assessment of *AdWeek*, the marketing industry bible: "Instagram's New Logo Is a Travesty. Can We Change It Back? Please?" In *GQ*'s article "Logo Change No One Wanted Just Came to Instagram," the magazine's panel of designers called the new icon "honestly horrible," "so ugly," and "trash," and summarized the change thus: "Instagram spent YEARS building up visual brand equity with its existing logo, training users where to tap, and now instead of iterating on that, it's flushing it all down the toilet for the homescreen equivalent of a Starburst."

Facebook *was not the first (nor the last) company* to experience such a reaction to a rebranding or a relaunch. PepsiCo experienced much the same with its aspartame-free Diet Pepsi—like the infamous New Coke debacle, a botched attempt at reinvention that translated into serious revenue losses and had to be reversed. The interesting question, therefore, is: Why do well-performing companies like these routinely succumb to the lure of radical rebranding? One could understand the temptation to adopt such a strategy in the face of disaster, but Instagram, PepsiCo, and Coke were hardly staring into the abyss. (It's worth noting that Snapchat, whose market share among young users is now particularly strong, has assiduously stuck to its familiar ghost icon.)

The answer, I believe, is rooted in some serious misperceptions about the nature of competitive advantage. Much of the latest thinking in strategy argues that the fast pace of change in modern business (perhaps nowhere more obvious than in the app world) means no competitive advantage is sustainable. In this worldview, companies need to continually update and adapt their business models, strategies, and communications in order to respond in real time to the explosion of choice that ever more sophisticated consumers now face. To keep customers loyal—and to attract new ones—you need to remain relevant and superior. Hence Instagram was doing exactly what it was supposed to do: changing proactively.

That's an edgy thought, to be sure, but a lot of evidence contradicts it. Consider Southwest Airlines, Vanguard, and IKEA, all featured in Michael Porter's classic 1996 HBR article "What Is Strategy?" as exemplars of long-lived competitive advantage as of twenty-five years ago. The notion that sustainable advantage is impossible notwithstanding, a full quarter century later all these companies are still at the top of their respective industries, pursuing largely unchanged strategies and branding. And although Google, Facebook, or Amazon might stumble and be crushed by some upstart, their competitive positions hardly look fleeting. The Tide or Head & Shoulders brand managers of the past seventy-five and sixty years, respectively, would certainly be surprised to hear that their greater-than-half-century advantages have not been or are not sustainable. And this brings me to an important truth about customers: *the familiar solution usually trumps the perfect one.*

In this chapter I'll draw on modern behavioral research to offer a theory that explains both missteps like Instagram's and success stories like Tide's. My argument is that sustained performance is achieved not by always offering customers the perfect choice but, rather, by offering them the easy one. So even if a value proposition is what attracted them in the first place, it is not necessarily what keeps them coming. In this alternative worldview, keeping customers loyal is not about continually adapting to changing needs in order to remain the rational or emotional best fit. It's about helping customers avoid having to make a choice. To do that, you have to create what I call *cumulative advantage.*

Let's begin by exploring what our brains actually do when we shop.

Creatures of Habit

The conventional wisdom about competitive advantage is that successful companies pick a position, target a set of consumers, and configure activities to serve them better. The goal is to make customers repeat their purchases by matching the value proposition to their needs. By fending off competitors through ever-evolving uniqueness and personalization, the company can achieve sustainable competitive advantage.

An assumption implicit in that definition is that consumers are making deliberate, perhaps even rational, decisions—their reasons for buying products and services may be emotional, but they always result from somewhat conscious logic. Therefore, a good strategy figures out and responds to that logic.

But the idea that purchase decisions arise from conscious choice flies in the face of much research in behavioral psychology. The brain, it turns out, is not so much an analytical machine as a gap-filling machine: it takes noisy, incomplete information from the world and quickly *fills in* the missing pieces on the basis of past experience. Intuition— thoughts, opinions, and preferences that come to mind quickly and without reflection but are strong enough to act on—is the end product of this process. It's not just *what* gets filled in that determines our intuitive judgments. They are heavily influenced by the speed and ease of the filling-in process itself, a phenomenon psychologists call *processing fluency*. When we describe making a decision because it "just feels right," the processing leading to the decision has been fluent.

Processing fluency is itself the product of repeated experience, and it increases exponentially with the number of times we have the experience. Perceiving and identifying an object is improved by prior exposure to that object. As an object is presented repeatedly, the neurons that code features not essential for recognizing the object dampen their responses and the neural network becomes more selective and efficient at object identification. Repeated stimuli have lower perceptual-identification thresholds, require less attention to be noticed, and are faster and more accurately named or read. What's more, consumers tend to prefer them to new stimuli.

In short, research into the workings of the human brain suggests that the mind loves automaticity more than just about anything else— certainly more than engaging in conscious consideration. Given a choice, it would like to do the same things again and again. If the mind develops a view over time that Tide gets clothes cleaner, and Tide is available and accessible on the store shelf or the web page, the easy, familiar thing to do is to buy Tide yet again.

A driving reason to choose the leading product in the market, there-fore, is simply that it is the easiest thing to do: in whatever distribution channel you shop, it will be the most prominent offering. In the supermarket, the mass merchandiser, or the drugstore, it will dominate the shelf. In addition, when you encounter the product in question, most likely you have bought it before from that very shelf. Doing so again is the easiest possible action to take. Not only that, but every time you buy another unit of the brand in question, you make it easier to do—for which the mind applauds you. That action contributes to a slight widening of the ease gap vis-à-vis the products you didn't choose, and that ease gap widens with every purchase and use. This logic holds as much in the new economy as in the old. If your browser is set to open Facebook as your home page, every aspect of which is totally familiar to you, the impact will be as powerful as facing a wall of Tide in a store—or more so.

Buying the biggest, easiest brand creates over time a cycle in which share leadership is continually increased. Each time you select and use a given product or service, its advantage cumulates over the products or services you didn't use.

The growth of cumulative advantage—absent changes that force conscious reappraisal—is inexorable. Thirty-five years ago, Tide enjoyed a small lead of 33 percent to 28 percent over Unilever's Surf in the lucrative US laundry detergent market. Consumers at the time slowly but surely formed habits that put Tide further ahead of Surf. Every year the habit differential increased, and the share gap widened. In 2008 Unilever exited the business and sold its brands to what was then a private-label detergent manufacturer. Now Tide enjoys a greater than 40 percent market share, making it the runaway market share leader in the US detergent market. Its largest branded competitor has a share of less than 10 percent. (For a discussion of why small brands even survive in this environment, see the sidebar "The Perverse Upside of Customer Disloyalty.")

The Perverse Upside of Customer Disloyalty

If consumers are slaves of habit, it's hard to argue that they are "loyal" customers in the sense that they consciously attach themselves to a brand on the assumption that it meets rational or emotional needs. In fact, customers are much more fickle than many marketers assume: often the brands that are believed to depend on loyal customers achieve the lowest loyalty scores.

For example, Colgate and Crest are the leading toothpaste brands in the US market, with about seventy-five share points between them. Customers for both are loyal 50 percent of the time (their preferred brand accounts for 50 percent of their annual toothpaste purchases). Tom's toothpaste, a niche "natural" brand based in Maine, has a 1 percent market share and is thought to have a fanatical customer following. One might expect the data to show that the 1 percent are mostly repeat buyers. But in fact, Tom's customers are loyal only 25 percent of the time—half the rate of the big brands.

So why do fringe brands like Tom's survive? The answer, perhaps perversely, is that with big-brand loyalty rates at 50 percent, just enough customers will buy small brands from time to time to keep the latter in business. But the small brands can't overcome the familiarity barrier, and although entirely new brands do enter categories and become leaders, it is extremely rare for an established fringe brand to successfully take on an established leader.

A Complement to Choice

I don't claim that consumer choice is never conscious, or that the quality of a value proposition is irrelevant. To the contrary: people have to have a reason to buy a product in the first place. And sometimes a new technology or a new regulation enables a company to demand consideration of a product—by radically lowering the price, offering new features, or providing a wholly new solution to a customer need.

Robust where-to-play and how-to-win choices, therefore, are still essential to strategy. Without a value proposition superior to those of competitors that are attempting to appeal to the same customers, a company has nothing to build on.

But if it is to extend that initial competitive advantage, the company must invest in turning its proposition into a habit rather than a choice. Hence, we can formally define cumulative advantage as the layer that a company builds on its initial competitive advantage by making its product or service an ever more instinctively comfortable choice for the customer.

Companies that fail to build cumulative advantage are likely to be overtaken by competitors that succeed in doing so. A good example is provided by MySpace, whose failure is often cited as proof that competitive advantage is inherently unsustainable. Let me present a different interpretation.

Launched in August 2003, MySpace became America's number one social networking site within two years and in 2006 overtook Google to become the most visited site of any kind in America. Nevertheless, a mere two years later, it was outstripped by Facebook, which demolished it competitively—so much so that MySpace was sold in 2011 for $35 million, a fraction of the $580 million NewsCorp had paid for it in 2005.

Why did MySpace fail? Our answer is that it didn't even try to achieve and sustain cumulative advantage. To begin with, it famously allowed users to create web pages that expressed their own personal style, so individual pages looked very different to visitors. It also placed advertising in jarring ways—and included ads for indecent services, which riled regulators. When NewsCorp bought MySpace, it ramped up ad density, further cluttering the site. In an attempt to entice more users, MySpace rolled out what *Bloomberg Businessweek* referred to as "a dizzying number of features: communication tools such as instant messaging, a classifieds program, a video player, a music player, a virtual karaoke machine, a self-serve advertising platform, profile-editing tools, security systems, privacy filters, MySpace book lists, and on and on." As a result, instead of making its site an ever more comfortable and instinctive choice, MySpace kept its users off balance, wondering (if not subconsciously worrying) what was coming next.

Compare that to Facebook. From day one, Facebook has been building cumulative advantage. Initially it had some attractive features that MySpace lacked, making it a good value proposition, but more important to its success has been the consistency of its look and feel. Users conform to rigid Facebook standards, and Facebook conforms to nothing or no one else. When it made its now-famous extension from desktop to mobile, Facebook ensured that users' mobile experience was highly consistent with their desktop experience. Its new service introductions do not jeopardize comfort and familiarity. By providing a reliably familiar experience, Facebook has built cumulative advantage to become the most addictive social networking site in the world. That makes its subsidiary Instagram's decision to change its icon all the more baffling.

The Cumulative Advantage Imperatives

MySpace and Facebook nicely illustrate the twin realities that sustainable advantage is both possible and not assured. How, then, might the next MySpace sustain, enhance, and extend its competitive advantage by building a protective layer of cumulative advantage? Here are four basic rules to follow.

Become popular early

This idea is far from new—it is implicit in many of the best and earliest works on strategy, and we can see it in the achievement of Bruce Henderson, the famous founder of Boston Consulting Group. Henderson's particular focus was on the beneficial impact of cumulative output on costs—the now-famous Experience Curve, which suggests that as experience in making something increases, the manufacturer's cost management becomes more efficient. He argued that companies should price aggressively early on—"ahead of the Experience Curve," in his parlance—and thus win enough market share to give the company lower costs, higher relative share, and higher profitability. The implication was clear: early share advantage matters—a lot.

Marketers have long understood the importance of winning early. Launched specifically to serve the fast-growing automatic washing machine market, Tide is one of P&G's most revered, successful, and profitable brands. When it was introduced, in 1946, it immediately had the heaviest advertising weight in the category. P&G also made sure that no automatic washing machine was sold in America without a free box of Tide to get consumers' habit started. Tide quickly won the early popularity contest and has never looked back.

Free new-product samples to gain trial have always been a popular tactic with marketers. Aggressive pricing is similarly popular. Samsung has emerged as the market share leader in the smartphone industry worldwide by providing very affordable Android-based phones that carriers can offer free with service contracts. For internet businesses, free is the core tactic for establishing habits. Virtually all the large-scale internet success stories—eBay, Google, Twitter, Instagram, Uber, Airbnb—make their services free to users to grow and deepen their habits and then sell those users to a provider or an advertiser willing to pay.

Design for habit

As we've seen, the best outcome is that your offering becomes the object of an automatic response. So, design for that—don't leave the outcome entirely to chance. We've seen how Facebook profits from its attention to consistent, habit-forming design, which has made use of its platform go beyond what we think of as habit: checking for updates has become a real addiction for a billion people. Of course, Facebook benefits from increasingly huge network effects. But the real advantage is that to switch from Facebook also entails breaking a powerful addiction.

The smartphone pioneer BlackBerry is perhaps the best example of a company that consciously designed for addiction. Its founder, Mike Lazaridis, explicitly created the device to make the cycle of feeling a buzz in the holster, slipping out the BlackBerry, checking the message, and thumbing a response on the miniature QWERTY keyboard as addictive as possible. He succeeded, earning the nickname CrackBerry for the device. The strength of the habit was so great that even after BlackBerry had been brought down by the move to internet app-based and touch-screen smartphones like the iPhone, a rump of heavily addicted BlackBerry customers—who had staunchly refused to adapt to the new habits—successfully implored the next generation of management to bring back a BlackBerry that resembled their previous-generation devices, with the comforting name Classic.

As Art Markman, a psychologist at the University of Texas, has pointed out, certain rules should be respected in designing for habit. To begin with, you must take care to keep consistent those elements of the product design that can be seen from a distance so that buyers can find your product quickly. Distinctive colors and shapes like Tide's bright orange and the Doritos logo accomplish this.

Find ways to make products fit in people's environments to encourage use. When P&G introduced Febreze, consumers liked the way it worked but did not use it often. Part of the problem, it turned out, was that the container was shaped like a glass-cleaner bottle, signaling that it should be kept under the sink. The bottle was ultimately redesigned to be kept on a counter or in a more visible cabinet and use after purchase increased.

Unfortunately, companies' design changes all too often end up disrupting habits rather than strengthening them. Look for changes that will reinforce habits and encourage repurchase. The Amazon Dash Button is an excellent example: by creating a simple way for people to reorder products they use often, Amazon helps them develop habits and locks them into a particular distribution channel.

Innovate inside the brand

As already noted, companies engage in initiatives to "relaunch," "repackage," or "replatform" at some peril—such efforts can require customers to break their habits. Of course, companies have to keep their products up to date, but changes in technology or other features should ideally be introduced in a manner that allows the new version of a product or service to take on cumulative advantage from the old.

Even the most successful builders of cumulative advantage sometimes forget this rule. P&G, for example, which has increased Tide's cumulative advantage over seventy-five years through huge changes, has had to learn some painful lessons along the way. Arguably the first great detergent innovation after Tide's launch was the creation of liquid detergents. P&G's first response was to launch a new brand, called Era, in 1975. With no cumulative advantage behind it, Era failed to become a major brand despite consumers' increasing substitution of liquid for powdered detergent.

Recognizing that as the number one brand in the category, Tide had a strong connection with consumers and a powerful cumulative advantage, P&G decided to launch Liquid Tide in 1984, in familiar packaging and with consistent branding. It went on to become the dominant liquid detergent despite its late entry. After that experience, P&G was careful to ensure that further innovations were consistent with the Tide brand. When its scientists figured out how to incorporate bleach into detergent, the product was called Tide plus Bleach. The breakthrough cold-cleaning technology appeared in Tide Coldwater, and the revolutionary three-in-one pod form was launched as Tide Pods. The branding could not have been simpler or clearer: this is your beloved Tide, with bleach added, for cold water, in pod form. These comfort- and familiarity-laden changes reinforced rather than diminished the brand's cumulative advantage. The new products all preserved the look of Tide's traditional packaging—the brilliant orange and the bull's-eye logo. The few times in Tide history when that look was altered—such as by blue packaging for the Tide Coldwater launch—the effect on consumers was significantly negative, and the change was quickly reversed.

Of course, sometimes change is absolutely necessary to maintain relevance and advantage. In such situations, smart companies succeed by helping customers transition from the old habit to the new one. Netflix began as a service that delivered DVDs to customers by mail. It would be out of business today if it had attempted to maximize continuity by refusing to change. Instead, it has successfully transformed itself into a video streaming service.

Although it now markets a completely different platform for digital entertainment, involving a new set of activities, Netflix has found ways to help its customers by accentuating what did not have to change. It has the same look and feel and is still a subscription service that gives people access to the latest entertainment without leaving their homes. Thus, its customers can deal with the necessary aspects of change while maintaining as much of the habit as possible. For customers, "improved" is much more comfortable and less scary than "new," however awesome "new" sounds to brand managers and advertising agencies.

Keep communication simple

One of the fathers of behavioral science, Daniel Kahneman, characterized subconscious, habit-driven decision-making as "thinking fast" and conscious decision-making as "thinking slow." Marketers and advertisers often seem to live in thinking-slow mode. They are rewarded with industry kudos for the cleverness with which they weave together and highlight the multiple benefits of a new product or service. True, ads that are clever and memorable sometimes move customers to change their habits. The slow-thinking conscious mind, if it decides to pay attention, may well say, "Wow, that is impressive. I can't wait!"

But if viewers aren't paying attention (as in the vast majority of cases), an artful communication may backfire. Consider an ad that came out for one of the iterations of Samsung's market-leading Galaxy smartphone. It began by showing successive vignettes of generic-looking smartphones failing to (a) demonstrate water resistance; (b) protect against a young child's accidentally sending an embarrassing message; and (c) enable an easy change of battery. It then triumphantly pointed out that the Galaxy, which looked pretty much like the three previous phones, overcomes all these flaws.

Conscious, slow-thinking viewers, if they watched the whole ad, may have been persuaded that the Galaxy in question was different from and superior to other phones. But an arguably greater likelihood was that fast-thinking viewers would subconsciously associate it with the three shortcomings. When making a purchase decision, they might be swayed by a subconscious plea: "Don't buy the one with the water-resistance, rogue-message, and battery-change problems." In fact, the ad might even induce them to buy a competitor's product—such as the iPhone—whose message about water resistance at the time was simpler to take in.

Remember: the mind is lazy. It doesn't want to ramp up attention to absorb a message with this level of complexity. Simply showing the water resistance of the Samsung Galaxy would have been much more powerful—or better yet, showing a customer buying a Galaxy and being told by the sales rep that it was fully water-resistant. The latter would tell fast-thinking minds what you wanted them to do: go to a store and buy the Samsung Galaxy. Of course, neither of those ads would be likely to win any awards from marketers focused on the cleverness of advertising copy.

• • •

Many strategists seem convinced that sustainable advantage can be delivered only by constantly making a company's value proposition the conscious consumer's rational or emotional first choice. They have forgotten, or never understood, the dominance of the subconscious mind in decision-making. For fast thinkers, products and services that are easy to access and that reinforce comfortable buying habits will over time trump innovative but unfamiliar alternatives that may be harder to find and require forming new habits. So, beware of falling into the trap of constantly updating your value proposition and branding. And whether it is a large established player, occupies a narrow niche within its market, or is a new entrant to a new market, any company can sustain the initial advantage provided by a superior value proposition by understanding and following the four rules of cumulative advantage.

This chapter is adapted from A.G. Lafley and Roger L. Martin, "Customer Loyalty Is Overrated," *Harvard Business Review*, January–February 2017.

PART TWO

Making Choices

4

Strategy

In strategy, what counts is what would
have to be true—not what is true.

S trategic planners pride themselves on their rigor. Strategies
are supposed to be driven by numbers and extensive analysis
and uncontaminated by bias, judgment, or opinion. The larger
the spreadsheets, the more confident an organization is in its process.
All those numbers, all those analyses, *feel* scientific, and in the modern
world, "scientific" equals "good."

Yet if that's the case, why do the operations managers in most large
and midsize firms dread the annual strategic planning ritual? Why
does it consume so much time and have so little impact on company
actions? Talk to those managers, and you will most likely uncover a
deeper frustration: the sense that strategic planning does not produce
novel strategies. Instead, it perpetuates the status quo.

One common reaction is to become explicitly antiscientific—to
throw off the shackles of organized number crunching and resort to
off-site "ideation events" or online "jam sessions" intended to promote
"out of the box" thinking. These processes may result in radical new

ideas, but more likely than not, those ideas cannot be translated into strategic choices that guide productive action. As one manager put it, "There's a reason we keep those ideas outside the box."

To break through the impasse, you have to change the way you think about making a successful strategy: *In strategy, what counts is what would have to be true—not what is true.* To put it in scientific terms, developing a winning strategy involves the creation and testing of novel cause-effect hypotheses and the identification of what must be different about the world for those hypotheses to work. And a structured development of novel hypotheses is as much a scientific process as the structured analysis of data.

In this chapter I'll lay out a seven-step approach to strategy-making anchored in the structured formulation of a set of well-articulated hypotheses—or *strategic possibilities*—for strategists to choose between. It examines what would have to be true about the world for each possibility to be supported. Only then does it unleash the power of analysis to determine which of what-would-have-to-be-trues is most feasibly attainable.

Step 1: Move from Issues to Choice

Conventional strategy-making tends to focus on problems or issues, such as declining profits or market share. As long as this is the case, the organization will fall into the trap of investigating data related to the issues rather than exploring and testing possible solutions.

A simple way to get strategists to avoid that trap is to require them to define two mutually exclusive options that could resolve the issue in question. Once you have framed the problem as a choice—any choice—your analysis and emotions will focus on what you have to do next, not on describing or analyzing the challenge. The possibilities-based approach therefore begins with the recognition that the organization must make a choice and that the choice has consequences. For the management team, this is the proverbial crossing of the Rubicon—the step that starts the strategy-making process.

In the late 1990s, when Procter & Gamble was contemplating becoming a major player in the global beauty care sector, it had a big issue: it lacked a credible brand in skin care, the largest and most profitable segment of the sector. All it had was Oil of Olay, a small, downmarket brand with an aging consumer base. P&G crossed its Rubicon and laid out two possibilities: it could attempt to dramatically transform Oil of Olay into a worthy competitor of brands like L'Oréal, Clarins, and La Prairie, or it could spend billions of dollars to buy a major existing skin care brand. This framing helped managers internalize the magnitude of what was at stake. At that point P&G turned from contemplating an issue to facing a serious choice.

Step 2: Generate Strategic Possibilities

Having recognized that a choice needs to be made, you can now turn to the full range of possibilities you should consider. These might be versions of the options already identified. For example, P&G could try to grow Oil of Olay in its current price tier or take it upmarket, or it could seek to buy the German company that owns Nivea or pry Clinique out of the hands of Estée Lauder. Possibilities might also exist outside the initial options. For instance, P&G could extend its successful cosmetics brand, Cover Girl, into skin care and build a global brand on that platform.

Constructing strategic possibilities, especially ones that are genuinely new, is the ultimate creative act in business. No one in the rest of the beauty industry would have imagined P&G's completely reinventing Olay and boldly going head-to-head against leading prestige brands. To generate such creative options, you need a clear idea of what constitutes a possibility. You also need an imaginative yet grounded team and a robust process for managing debate.

Desired output

A possibility is essentially a happy story that describes how a firm might succeed. Each story lays out where the company plays in its market and how it wins there. It should have internally consistent logic, but it need not be proved at this point. As long as we can imagine that it *could* be valid, it makes the cut. Characterizing possibilities as stories that do not require proof helps people discuss what might be viable but does not yet exist. It is much easier to tell a story about why a possibility could make sense than to provide data on the odds that it will succeed.

A common temptation is to sketch out possibilities only at the highest level. But a motto ("Go global") or a goal ("Be number one") does not constitute a strategic possibility. We push teams to specify in detail the *advantage* they aim to achieve or leverage, the *scope* across which the advantage applies, and the *activities* throughout the value chain that would deliver the intended advantage across the targeted scope. Otherwise, it is impossible to unpack the logic underlying a possibility and to subject the possibility to subsequent tests. In the Cover Girl possibility, the advantage would come from Cover Girl's strong brand and existing consumer base combined with Procter & Gamble's R&D and global go-to-market capabilities. The scope would be limited to the younger demographic at the heart of the current Cover Girl consumer base, and it would need to build internationally from North America, where the brand was strong. The key activities would include leveraging Cover Girl's stable of model and celebrity endorsers.

Managers often ask, "How many possibilities should we generate?" The answer varies according to context. Some industries offer few happy stories—there are simply not a lot of good alternatives. Others, particularly ones in ferment or with numerous customer segments, have many potential directions. I find that most teams consider three to five possibilities in depth. On one aspect of this question, I am adamant: the team *must* produce more than one possibility. Otherwise, it never really started the strategy-making process because it didn't see itself as facing a choice. Analyzing a single possibility is not conducive to producing optimal action—or, in fact, any action at all.

I also insist that the status quo or current trajectory be among the possibilities considered. This forces the team in later stages to specify what must be true for the status quo to be viable, thereby eliminating the common implicit assumption "Worst case, we can just keep doing what we're already doing." The status quo is sometimes a path to decline. By including it among the possibilities, a team makes it subject to investigation and potential doubt.

The team at P&G surfaced five strategic possibilities in addition to the status quo. One was to abandon Oil of Olay and acquire a major global skin care brand. A second was to keep Oil of Olay positioned where it was, as an entry-priced, mass-market brand, and to strengthen its appeal to current older consumers by leveraging R&D capabilities to improve its wrinkle-reduction performance. A third was to take Oil of Olay into the prestige distribution channel—department stores and specialty beauty shops—as an upscale brand. A fourth was to completely reinvent Olay as a prestige-like brand that would appeal more broadly to younger women (age thirty-five to fifty) but be sold in traditional mass channels by retail partners willing to create a "masstige" experience, with a special display section. A fifth was to extend the Cover Girl brand to skin care.

The people

The group tasked with dreaming up strategic possibilities should represent a diversity of specialties, backgrounds, and experiences.

Otherwise, it is difficult to generate creative possibilities and to flesh out each one in sufficient detail. I find it useful to include individuals who did not create, and therefore are not emotionally bound to, the status quo. This usually implies that promising junior executives will participate. I also find that individuals from outside the firm, preferably outside the industry, often lend the most original ideas. Finally, I believe it's crucial to include operations managers, not just staff members, in the process. This not only deepens practical wisdom but also builds early commitment to and knowledge of the strategy that is ultimately chosen. If you show me a company where the planners are different from the doers, I will show you a company where what gets done is different from what was planned.

Optimal group size varies among organizations and their cultures. Companies with a culture of inclusion, for example, should assemble a large group. If you go this route, use breakout groups to discuss the specific possibilities; a group larger than eight or ten people tends to be self-censoring.

It's usually not a good idea to have the most senior person serve as the leader; she will have a difficult time convincing the others that she is not playing her usual role as boss. Instead, choose a respected lower-level insider who is not perceived as having a strong point of view on which course should be chosen. Or tap an outside facilitator who has some experience with the firm.

The rules

Once selected, the possibility generators must commit themselves to separating their first step—the creation of possibilities—from the subsequent steps of testing and selecting. Managers with critical minds naturally tend to greet each new idea with a long list of reasons why it won't work. The leader must constantly remind the group that ample time for

skepticism will come later; for now, it must suspend judgment. If anyone persists with a critique, the leader should require him to reframe it
as a condition and table it for discussion in the next step. For example,
the critique "Customers will never accept differential pricing" becomes
the condition "This possibility requires that customers accept differential pricing." It's particularly important that the leader not shoot down
possibilities early. If that happens, it's open season on all possibilities.
And removing an option about which a particular team member feels
strongly may cause that person to withdraw from the process.

Many management teams try to generate strategic possibilities in a
single off-site brainstorming session. Such sessions are useful, especially if they are held at an unusual location that gets people out of their
accustomed routines and habits of mind. But I have also seen teams
benefit from spreading the possibility-generation process over some
time so that individuals have an opportunity to reflect, think creatively,
and build on ideas. It is perhaps most effective to start by asking each
person to spend thirty to forty-five minutes sketching out three to five
(or more) stories. The stories do not need to be detailed; they should
truly be sketches. After this exercise the group (or breakout groups)
fleshes out the initial possibilities.

Possibility generation centers on creativity, and many techniques
purport to boost creativity. I've found three kinds of probing questions to be especially useful. *Inside-out* questions start with the company's assets and capabilities and then reason outward: What does this
company do especially well that parts of the market might value and
that might produce a superior wedge between buyer value and costs?
Outside-in questions look for openings in the market: What are the
underserved needs, what are the needs that customers find hard to
express, and what gaps have competitors left? *Far-outside-in* questions
use analogical reasoning: What would it take to be the Google, the
Apple, or the Walmart of this market?

You will know that you have a good set of possibilities for further work if two things prove to be true. First, the status quo doesn't look like a brilliant idea: At least one other possibility intrigues the group enough to make it really question the existing order. Second, at least one possibility makes most of the group uncomfortable: It is sufficiently far from the status quo that the group questions whether it would be at all doable or safe. If one or both of these don't hold, it is probably time for another round of possibility generation.

The uncomfortable possibility for P&G was the fourth option described above. It involved transforming a weak, low-end brand into a more desirable player that could compete with upmarket department store products and then creating an entirely new masstige segment that mass retailers would enthusiastically support.

Step 3: Specify the Conditions for Success

The purpose of this step is to specify what *must be true* for each possibility to be a terrific choice. Note that this step is not intended for arguing about what *is* true. It is not intended to explore or assess the soundness of the logic behind the various possibilities or to consider data that may or may not support the logic—that comes later. Any consideration of evidence at this point detracts from the process.

The importance of this distinction cannot be overstated. When the discussion of a possibility centers on *what is true*, the person most skeptical about the possibility attacks it vigorously, hoping to knock it out of contention. The originator defends it, parrying arguments in order to protect its viability. Tempers rise, statements become more extreme, and relationships are strained. Meanwhile, little of either opponent's logic is revealed to the other.

If, instead, the dialogue is about *what would have to be true*, then the skeptic can say, "For me to be confident in this possibility,

I would have to know that consumers will embrace this sort of offering." That is a very different sort of statement from "That will never work!" It helps the proponent understand the skeptic's reservations and develop the proof to overcome them. It also makes the skeptic specify the exact source of the skepticism rather than issue a blanket denunciation.

I've helped develop a process for surfacing the conditions that have to be true for a possibility to be an attractive strategy (see the sidebar "Assessing the Validity of a Strategic Option"). The conditions fall into seven categories relating to the industry, customer value, business model, and competitors. Managers should begin by clearly spelling out the strategic possibility under consideration before moving to a two-stage discussion.

Generate a list

The aim here is to enumerate all the conditions that need to hold true for everyone in the room to be able to honestly say, "I feel confident enough to make this possibility a reality." The conditions should be expressed as declarative rather than conditional statements—for example, "Channel partners will support us," not "Channel partners would have to support us." This helps paint a positive picture of the possibility, one that will be inviting to the group if the conditions actually hold.

You must make sure that the individual who proposed the possibility under review does not dominate this conversation. Any condition that is put forward should be added to the list. The person putting it forward should simply be asked to explain why that condition would be necessary for him to be confident; he should not be challenged about the truth of the condition.

When each member of the group has had a chance to add conditions to the list, the facilitator should read the list aloud and ask the

Assessing the Validity of a Strategic Option

Once you've listed all your options, specify what must be true for each to succeed. The diagram provides a framework for surfacing the necessary conditions; in effect, you are reverse engineering your choice. P&G's application of the framework to its option for a renamed and repositioned Olay is shown at the end.

The Framework

In order to pursue this option successfully, what conditions would we have to believe existed or could be created?

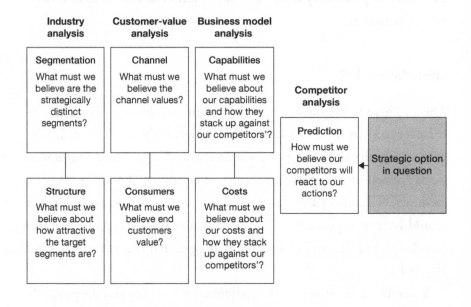

The Olay "Masstige" Option

The option under consideration was to reposition Olay for a younger demographic, with the promise to "fight the seven signs of aging." It would involve partnering with retailers to create a masstige segment—consumers willing to buy a prestige-like product in mass channels. P&G determined that for this option to succeed, these conditions would have to exist or be created.

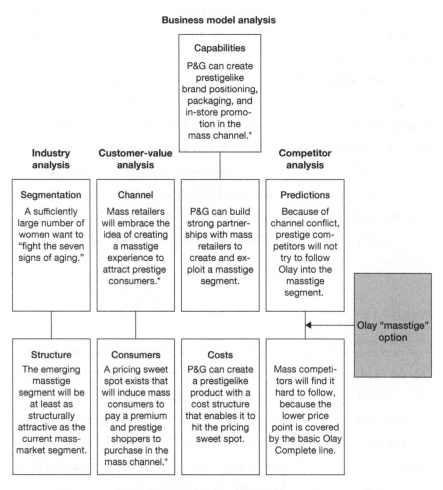

Business model analysis

Capabilities
P&G can create prestigelike brand positioning, packaging, and in-store promotion in the mass channel.*

Industry analysis

Customer-value analysis

Competitor analysis

Segmentation	Channel		Predictions
A sufficiently large number of women want to "fight the seven signs of aging."	Mass retailers will embrace the idea of creating a masstige experience to attract prestige consumers.*	P&G can build strong partnerships with mass retailers to create and exploit a masstige segment.	Because of channel conflict, prestige competitors will not try to follow Olay into the masstige segment.

Olay "masstige" option

Structure	Consumers	Costs	
The emerging masstige segment will be at least as structurally attractive as the current mass-market segment.	A pricing sweet spot exists that will induce mass consumers to pay a premium and prestige shoppers to purchase in the mass channel.*	P&G can create a prestigelike product with a cost structure that enables it to hit the pricing sweet spot.	Mass competitors will find it hard to follow, because the lower price point is covered by the basic Olay Complete line.

* Barrier conditions: the ones P&G thought least likely to hold true

group, "If all these conditions were true, would you advocate for and support this choice?" If everyone says yes, it's time to move to the next step. If any members say no, they must be asked, "What additional condition would enable you to answer yes?" This line of questioning should continue until every member replies affirmatively.

Once again, during this step, expressing opinions about whether or not conditions are true should be strictly prohibited. The point is simply to ferret out *what would have to be true* for every member of the group to feel cognitively and emotionally committed to each possibility under consideration.

It is important to treat the current strategy in this way as well. I recall one discussion a number of years ago about the status quo option. Toward the end, the president of the company leaped out of his seat and sprinted from the room. When he returned, ten minutes later, his colleagues asked whether he was OK. He explained that the discussion had made him see how logically weak the status quo was. The reason he had raced out was to cancel a multimillion-dollar initiative in support of the status quo—the go/no-go deadline was that very day.

Weed the list

The previous exercise typically overshoots, and the list of conditions crosses the line between "must have" and "nice to have." After finishing the list of conditions, the group should take a break and then review the items, asking, "If every condition but this one held true, would you eliminate the possibility or still view it as viable?" If the answer is the former, the condition is a must-have and should be maintained. If it is the latter, it is a nice-to-have and should be removed.

The goal here is to ensure that the list of conditions is truly a binding set. To this end, once you're finished reviewing, you should ask, "If all these conditions were true, would you advocate for and support this choice?" If any member says no, then the group needs to return to the first-stage discussion and add any necessary conditions that were initially overlooked or mistakenly removed.

After arriving at a full set of possibilities and ensuring that all must-have conditions are attached to each, the group needs to bring its options to the executives whose approval will be required to ratify the final choice and to any other colleagues who might stand in the way. For each possibility, the group needs to ask these people the same questions it asked its members: "If these conditions were shown to hold true, would you choose this possibility? If not, what additional conditions would you include?" The goal is to make sure that the conditions for each possibility are well specified in the eyes of everyone with a say in the choice—*before* analysis ensues.

Step 4: Identify the Barriers to Choice

Now it's time to cast a critical eye on the conditions. The task is to assess which ones you believe are least likely to hold true. They will define the barriers to choosing that possibility.

Begin by asking group members to imagine that they could buy a guarantee that any particular condition will hold true. To which condition would they apply it? The condition they choose is, by inference, the biggest barrier to choosing the possibility under consideration. The next condition to which they would apply a guarantee is the next-biggest barrier, and so on. The ideal output is an ordered list of barriers to each possibility, two or three of which really worry the group. If there is disagreement about the ordering of particular conditions, you should rank them as equal.

Pay close attention to the member who is most skeptical that a given condition will hold true; that person represents the greatest obstacle—and, in the case of a problematic possibility, an extremely valuable obstacle—to the selection and pursuit of the option. Members must be encouraged to raise, not suppress, their concerns. Even if only one person is concerned about a given condition, the condition must be kept on the list. Otherwise, he would be within his rights to dismiss the final analysis. If the skepticism of every member is drawn out and taken seriously, all will feel confident in the process and the outcomes.

When the P&G beauty care team reviewed the nine conditions it had come up with for the Olay masstige possibility, the members felt confident that six would hold: the potential consumer segment was big enough to be worth targeting; the segment was at least as structurally attractive as the current mass-market skin care segment; P&G could produce the product at a cost that would permit a somewhat lower price than those of key lower-end prestige players; it was capable of building retailer partnerships (if retailers liked the idea); prestige competitors would not copy the strategy; and mass competitors could not copy the strategy. However, three conditions worried the team, in descending order: that mass-channel consumers would accept a new, significantly higher starting price point; that mass-channel players would be game to create a new masstige segment; and that P&G could bring together prestige-like brand positioning, product packaging, and in-store promotion elements in the mass-retail channel.

Step 5: Design Tests for the Barrier Conditions

Once you've identified and ordered the key barrier conditions, the group must test each one to see whether it holds true. The test might involve surveying a thousand customers or speaking to a single supplier. It might entail crunching thousands of numbers or avoiding any quantifiers at all. The only requirement is that the entire group believe that the test is valid and can form the basis for rejecting the possibility in question or generating commitment to it.

The member who is most skeptical about a given condition should take the lead in designing and applying the test for it. This person will typically have the highest standard of proof; if she is satisfied that the condition has passed the test, everyone else will be satisfied. The risk, of course, is that the skeptic might set an unachievable standard. In practice this does not happen, for two reasons.

First, people demonstrate extreme skepticism largely because they don't feel heard. In a typical buy-in process, concerns are treated as road blocks to be pushed aside as quickly as is feasible. The possibilities-based approach ensures that individuals with concerns both feel and actually are heard. The second reason is the specter of mutually assured destruction. Though I may have serious doubts about possibility A, I quite like possibility B. You, on the other hand, have few doubts about possibility A but have serious qualms about choosing possibility B. I get to set the tests for the barrier conditions for possibility A, but I do so with the knowledge that you will be setting the tests for possibility B. If I set too high a bar, you will surely do the same. Being fair and sensible is, then, the smartest approach.

Step 6: Conduct the Tests

I typically advise structuring this step according to what I call "the lazy person's approach to choice," testing conditions in the reverse order of the group's confidence. That is, the condition the group feels is least likely to hold up is tested first. If the group's suspicion is right, the possibility at hand can be eliminated without any further testing. If that condition passes the test, the condition with the next-lowest likelihood of confirmation is tested, and so on. Because testing is often the most expensive and time-consuming part of the process, the lazy person's approach can save enormous resources.

Typically, at this step you bring in people from outside the strategy team—consultants or experts in relevant functional or geographic units who can help fine-tune and conduct the tests you have prioritized. It is important to ensure that they concentrate solely on testing. You are not asking them to revisit the conditions. In fact, one beauty of the possibilities-based approach is that it enables you to focus outside resources that may be costly and time-consuming.

This approach differs profoundly from the process followed by most strategy consultants, who conduct a relatively standard suite of analyses in parallel. That generates a lot of (expensive) analysis, much of which turns out to be not essential or even useful in decision-making. Furthermore, depth is sacrificed for breadth: analyses are a mile wide and an inch deep because the cost of deep analysis across the board would be prohibitive. To generate choice and commitment, managers need analysis that is an inch wide and a mile deep—targeting the concerns that could prevent the group from choosing an option and exploring those areas thoroughly enough to meet the group's standard of proof. The possibilities-based approach permits this.

For the P&G beauty care team, the most challenging condition for the Olay masstige possibility related to pricing. The test of the condition showcased the ability of a truly scientific, hypothesis-driven approach to generate strategies that are both unexpected and successful. Joe Listro, Olay's R&D manager, explains how it went. "We started to test the new Olay product at premium price points of $12.99 to $18.99 and got very different results," he says. "At $12.99, there was a positive response and a reasonably good rate of purchase intent. But most who signaled a desire to buy at $12.99 were mass shoppers. Very few department store shoppers were interested at that price point. Basically, we were trading people up from within the channel. At $15.99, purchase intent dropped dramatically. At $18.99, it went back up again—way up. So, $12.99 was really good, $15.99 not so good, $18.99 great."

The team learned that at $18.99, consumers were crossing over from prestige department and specialty stores to buy Olay in discount, drug, and grocery stores. That price point sent exactly the right message. For the department store shopper, the product was a great value but still credibly expensive. For the mass shopper, the premium price signified that the product must be considerably better than anything else on the shelf. In contrast, $15.99 was in no-man's land—for a mass shopper, expensive without signaling differentiation, and for a prestige shopper, not expensive enough. These differences were quite fine; had the team not focused so carefully on building and applying robust tests for multiple price points, the findings might never have emerged.

It is important to understand that tests cannot eliminate all uncertainty. Even the best-performing possibility will entail some risk. That is why it is so crucial to set testable conditions for the status quo: the team then clearly sees that the status quo is not free of risk. Rather than compare the best-performing possibility with a non-existent risk-free option, the team can compare the risk of the leading option with the risk of the status quo and reach a decision in that context.

Step 7: Make the Choice

In traditional strategy-making, finally choosing a strategy can be difficult and acrimonious. The decision makers usually go off-site and try to frame their binders of much-discussed market research as strategic options. With the stakes high and the logic for each option never clearly articulated, such meetings often end up as negotiations between powerful executives with strong preconceptions. And once the meetings are concluded, those who are skeptical of the decision begin to undermine it.

With the possibilities-based approach, the choice-making step becomes simple, even anticlimactic. The group needs only to review the analytical test results and choose the possibility that faces the fewest serious barriers.

Often a strategy chosen in this way is surprisingly bold and would most likely have been strangled at birth in the traditional process. Consider the Olay case. P&G ended up deciding to launch an upmarket product called Olay Total Effects for $18.99. In other words, the brand once dismissed as "Oil for Old Ladies" was transformed into a prestige-like product line at a price point close to that of department store brands. And it worked. Mass-retail partners loved the product and saw new shoppers buying at new price points in their stores. Beauty magazine editors and dermatologists saw real value in the well-priced, effective product line.

The masstige strategy succeeded beyond expectations. P&G would have been happy with a billion-dollar global skin care brand. But in less than a decade, the Olay brand surpassed $2.5 billion in annual sales by spawning a series of "boutique" product lines—starting with Total Effects and following with Regenerist, Definity, and Pro-X—that attracted more prestige shoppers and commanded prices eventually reaching $50.

• • •

Laid out neatly on paper, the possibilities-based approach outlined here sounds easy. But many managers struggle with it—not because the mechanics are hard, but because the approach requires at least three fundamental shifts in mindset. First, in the early steps, they must avoid asking "What should we do?" and instead ask "What might we do?"

Managers, especially those who pride themselves on being decisive, jump naturally to the former question and get restless when tackling the latter.

Second, in the middle steps, managers must shift from asking "What do I believe?" to asking "What would I have to believe?" This requires a manager to imagine that each possibility, including ones he does not like, is a great idea, and such a mindset does not come naturally to most people. It's needed, however, to identify the right tests for a possibility.

Finally, by focusing a team on pinpointing the critical conditions and tests, the possibilities-based approach forces managers to move away from asking "What is the right answer?" and concentrate instead on "What are the right questions? What specifically must we know in order to make a good decision?" In our experience, most managers are better at advocacy of their own views than at inquiry, especially about others' views. The possibilities-based approach relies on and fosters a team's ability to inquire. And genuine inquiry must lie at the heart of any process that aims to be scientific.

This chapter is adapted from A.G. Lafley, Roger L. Martin, Jan W. Rivkin, and Nicolaj Siggelkow, "Bringing Science to the Art of Strategy," *Harvard Business Review*, September–October 2012.

5

Data

Creating great choices requires imagination more than data.

U nderlying the practice and study of business is the belief that business decisions must be driven by rigorous analysis of data. The explosion of big data has reinforced this idea. In a recent EY survey, 81 percent of executives said they believed that "data should be at the heart of all decision-making," leading EY to enthusiastically proclaim that "big data can eliminate reliance on 'gut feel' decision-making."

Managers find this notion appealing. Many have a background in applied sciences. Even if they don't, chances are, they have an MBA—a degree that originated in the early twentieth century, when Frederick Winslow Taylor was introducing "scientific management."

MBA programs now flood the business world with graduates—more than 150,000 a year in the United States alone. These programs have been trying to turn management into a hard science for most of the past six decades. In large measure this effort began in response to scathing reports on the state of business education in America issued by the Ford and Carnegie Foundations in 1959. In the view of the report writers—all economists—business programs were filled with underqualified students whose professors resisted the methodological rigor of the hard sciences, which other social sciences like economics had embraced. In short, business education wasn't scientific enough. It was in part to remedy this shortcoming that the Ford Foundation supported the creation of academic journals and funded the establishment of doctoral programs at Harvard Business School, the Carnegie Institute of Technology (the predecessor of Carnegie Mellon), Columbia, and the University of Chicago.

But has the pendulum gone too far in this direction? Can management decisions really be reduced to an exercise in data analysis? I do not believe that they can, and this brings me to an important truth about data: *creating great choices requires imagination more than data.* To understand what this means and why it is true, let's take a look back at where—or rather with whom—science started.

Is Business a Science?

What we think of as science began with Aristotle, who as a student of Plato was the first to write about cause and effect and the methodology for demonstrating it. This made "demonstration," or proof, the goal of science and the final criterion for "truth." As such, Aristotle was the originator of the approach to scientific exploration, which Galileo, Bacon, Descartes, and Newton would formalize as "the scientific method" two thousand years later.

It's hard to overestimate the impact of science on society. The scientific discoveries of the Enlightenment—deeply rooted in the Aristotelian methodology—led to the Industrial Revolution and the global economic progress that followed. Science solved problems and made the world a better place. Small wonder that we came to regard great scientists like Einstein as latter-day saints. And even smaller wonder that we came to view the scientific method as a template for other forms of inquiry and to speak of "social sciences" rather than "social studies."

But Aristotle might question whether we've allowed our application of the scientific method to go too far. In defining his approach, he set clear boundaries around what it should be used for, which was understanding natural phenomena that "cannot be other than they are." Why does the sun rise every day, why do lunar eclipses happen when they do, why do objects always fall to the ground? These things are beyond the control of any human, and science is the study of what makes them occur.

However, Aristotle never claimed that all events were inevitable. To the contrary, he believed in free will and the power of human agency to make choices that can radically change the future. In other words, people choose a great many things in the world that can be other than they are. "Most of the things about which we make decisions, and into which we therefore inquire, present us with alternative possibilities. . . . All our actions have a contingent character; hardly any of them are determined by necessity," he wrote. He believed that this realm of possibilities was driven not by scientific analysis but by human invention and persuasion.

This is particularly true when it comes to decisions about business strategy and innovation. You can't chart a course for the future or bring about change merely by analyzing history. The behavior of customers will never be transformed by a product whose design is based on an analysis of their past behavior.

Yet transforming customer habits and experiences is what great business innovations do. Steve Jobs, Steve Wozniak, and other computing pioneers created a brand-new device that revolutionized how people interacted and did business. The railroad, the motor car, and the telephone all introduced enormous behavioral and social shifts that an analysis of prior data could not have predicted. To be sure, innovators often incorporate scientific discoveries in their creations, but their real genius lies in their ability to imagine products or processes that simply never existed before.

The real world is not merely an outcome determined by ineluctable laws of science; to act as if it is denies the possibility of genuine innovation. A purely scientific approach to business decision-making has serious limitations, and managers need to figure out where those limitations lie.

Can or Cannot?

Most situations involve some elements you can change and some you cannot. The critical skill is spotting the difference. The question you need to ask is this: Is the situation dominated by possibility (that is, things we can alter for the better) or by necessity (elements we cannot change)?

Suppose you plan to build a bottling line for plastic bottles of spring water. The standard way to set one up is to take "forms" (miniature thick plastic tubes), heat them, use air pressure to mold them to full bottle size, cool them until they're rigid, and finally fill them with water. Thousands of bottling lines around the world are configured this way.

Some of this cannot be other than it is: how hot the form has to be to stretch; the amount of air pressure required to mold the bottle; how fast the bottle can be cooled; how quickly the water can fill the bottle. These are determined by the laws of thermodynamics and gravity—which executives cannot do a thing to change.

Still, there's an awful lot they can change. While the laws of science govern each step, the steps themselves don't have to follow the sequence that has dominated bottling for decades. A company called LiquiForm demonstrated that after asking: Why can't we combine two steps into one by forming the bottle with pressure from the liquid we're putting into it, rather than using air? And that idea turned out to be utterly doable.

Executives need to deconstruct every decision-making situation into *cannot* and *can* parts and then test their logic. If the initial hypothesis is that an element can't be changed, the executive needs to ask what laws of nature suggest this. If the rationale for *cannot* is compelling, then the best approach is to apply a methodology that will optimize the status quo. In that case let science be the master and use its tool kits of data and analytics to drive choices.

In a similar way, executives need to test the logic behind classifying elements as *cans*. What suggests that behaviors or outcomes can be different from what they have been? If the supporting rationale is strong enough, let design and imagination be the master and use analytics in their service.

It's important to realize that the presence of data is not sufficient proof that outcomes cannot be different. Data is not logic. In fact, many of the most lucrative business moves come from bucking the evidence. Lego Brand Group chair Jørgen Vig Knudstorp offers a case in point. Back in 2008, when he was the company's CEO, its data suggested that girls were much less interested in its toy bricks than boys were: 85 percent of Lego players were boys, and every attempt to attract more girls had failed. Many of the firm's managers, therefore, believed that girls were inherently less likely to play with the bricks—they saw it as a *cannot* situation. But Knudstorp did not. The problem, he thought, was that Lego had not yet figured out how to inspire girls to play with construction toys. His hunch was borne out with the launch of the successful Lego Friends line in 2012.

The Lego case illustrates that data is no more than evidence, and it's not always obvious what it is evidence of. Moreover, the absence of data does not preclude possibility. If you are talking about new outcomes and behaviors, then naturally there is no prior evidence. A truly rigorous thinker, therefore, considers not only what the data suggests but also what within the bounds of possibility could happen. And that requires the exercise of imagination—a very different process from analysis.

Also, the division between *can* and *cannot* is more fluid than most people think. Innovators will push that boundary more than most, challenging the *cannot*.

Breaking the Frame

The imagination of new possibilities first requires an act of unframing. The status quo often appears to be the only way things can be, a perception that's hard to shake.

I recently came across a good example of the status quo trap while advising a consulting firm whose clients are nonprofit organizations. The latter face a "starvation cycle," in which they get generously funded for the direct costs of specific programs but struggle to get support for their indirect costs. A large private foundation, for instance, may fully fund the expansion of a charity's successful Latin American girls' education program to sub-Saharan Africa, yet underwrite only a small fraction of the associated operational overhead and of the cost of developing the program in the first place. This is because donors typically set low and arbitrary levels for indirect costs—usually allowing only 10 percent to 15 percent of grants to go toward them, even though the true indirect costs make up 40 percent to 60 percent of the total tab for most programs.

The consulting firm accepted this framing of the problem and believed that the strategic challenge was figuring out how to persuade donors to increase the percentage allocated to indirect costs. It was considered a given that donors perceived indirect costs to be a necessary evil that diverted resources away from end beneficiaries.

I got the firm's partners to test that belief by listening to what donors said about costs rather than selling donors a story about the need to raise reimbursement rates. What the partners heard surprised them. Far from being blind to the starvation cycle, donors hated it and understood their own role in causing it. The problem was that they didn't trust their grantees to manage indirect costs. Once the partners were liberated from their false belief, they soon came up with a wide range of process-oriented solutions that could help nonprofits build their competence at cost management and earn their donors' confidence.

Although listening to and empathizing with stakeholders might not seem as rigorous or systematic as analyzing data from a formal survey, it is in fact a tried-and-true method of gleaning insights, familiar to anthropologists, ethnographers, sociologists, psychologists, and other social scientists. Many business leaders, particularly those who apply design thinking and other user-centric approaches to innovation, recognize the importance of qualitative, observational research in understanding human behavior. At Lego, for example, Knudstorp's initial questioning of gender assumptions triggered four years of ethnographic studies that led to the discovery that girls are more interested in collaborative play than boys are, which suggested that a collaborative construction toy could appeal to them.

Powerful tool though it is, ethnographic research is no more than the starting point for a new frame. Ultimately, you have to chart out what could be and get people on board with that vision. To do that, you need to create a new narrative that displaces the old frame that has confined people. And the story-making process has principles that are entirely different from the principles of natural science. Natural science explains the world as it is, but a story can describe a world that does not yet exist.

Constructing Persuasive Narratives

It may seem unlikely, but Aristotle, the same philosopher who gave us the scientific method, also set out methods for creating compelling narratives. In *The Art of Rhetoric*, he describes a system of persuasion that has three drivers:

- Ethos: the will and character to change the current situation. To be effective, the author of the narrative must possess credibility and authenticity.

- Logos: the logical structure of the argument. This must provide a rigorous case for transforming problems into possibilities, possibilities into ideas, and ideas into action.

- Pathos: the capacity to empathize. To be capable of inspiring movement on a large scale, the author must understand the audience.

A multibillion-dollar merger of two large insurance companies offers an example of how to use ethos, logos, and pathos. The two firms were longtime competitors. There were winners and losers in the deal, and employees at all levels were nervous and unsettled. To complicate matters, both firms had grown by acquisition, so in effect this was a merger of twenty or thirty different cultures. These smaller legacy groups had been independent and would resist efforts to integrate them to capture synergies. On top of that, the global financial crisis struck just after the merger, shrinking the industry by 8 percent. So, the merged enterprise's leaders faced a double challenge: a declining market and a skeptical organizational culture.

The normal approach to post-merger integration is rational and reductionist: analyze the current cost structures of the two organizations and combine them into one smaller structure—with the attendant layoffs of "redundant" employees. However, the leader of the merged companies did not want to follow the usual drill. Rather, he wanted to build a new organization from the ground up. He supplied the ethos by articulating the goal of accomplishing something bigger and better than a standard merger integration.

However, he needed the logos—a powerful and compelling case for a future that was different. He built one around the metaphor of a thriving city. Like a city, the new organization would be a diverse ecosystem that would grow in both planned and unplanned ways. Everybody would be part of that growth and contribute to the city. The logic of a thriving city captured the imagination of employees enough for them to lean into the task and imagine possibilities for themselves and their part of the organization.

The effort also required pathos—forging an emotional connection that would get employees to commit to building this new future together. To enlist them, the leadership group took a new approach to communication. Typically, executives communicate post-merger integration plans with town halls, presentations, and emails that put employees on the receiving end of messages. Instead, the leadership group set up a series of collaborative sessions in which units in the company held conversations about the thriving-city metaphor and used it to explore challenges and design the work in their sphere of activity. How would the claims department look different in the thriving city? What would finance look like? In effect, employees were creating their own mini narratives within the larger narrative the leaders had constructed. This approach required courage because it was so unusual and playful for such a large organization in a conservative industry.

The approach was a resounding success. Within six months, employee engagement scores had risen from a dismal 48 percent to a spectacular 90 percent. That translated into performance: while the industry shrank, the company's business grew by 8 percent, and its customer satisfaction scores rose from an average of 6 to 9 (on a scale of 1 to 10).

This case illustrates the importance of another rhetorical tool: a strong metaphor that captures the arc of your narrative in a sentence. A well-crafted metaphor reinforces all three elements of persuasion. It makes logos, the logical argument, more compelling and strengthens pathos by helping the audience connect to that argument. And finally, a more compelling and engaging argument enhances the moral authority and credibility of the leader—the ethos.

Picking the Right Metaphor

We all know that good stories are anchored by powerful metaphors. Aristotle himself observed, "Ordinary words convey only what we know already; it is from metaphor that we can best get hold of something fresh." In fact, he believed that mastery of metaphor was the key to rhetorical success: "To be a master of metaphor is the greatest thing by far. It is . . . a sign of genius," he wrote.

It's perhaps ironic that this proposition about an unscientific construct has been scientifically confirmed. Research in cognitive science has demonstrated that the core engine of creative synthesis is "associative fluency"—the mental ability to connect two concepts that are not usually linked and to forge them into a new idea. The more diverse the concepts, the more powerful the creative association and the more novel the new idea.

With a new metaphor, you compare two things that aren't usually connected. For instance, when Hamlet says to Rosencrantz, "Denmark's a prison," he is associating two elements in an unusual way. Rosencrantz knows what "Denmark" means, and he knows what "a prison" is. However, Hamlet presents a new concept to him that is neither the Denmark he knows nor the prisons he knows. This third element is the novel idea or creative synthesis produced by the unusual combination.

When people link unrelated concepts, product innovations often result. Samuel Colt developed the revolving bullet chamber for his famous pistol after working on a ship as a young man and becoming fascinated by the vessel's wheel and the way it could spin or be locked by means of a clutch. A Swiss engineer was inspired to create the hook-and-loop model of Velcro after walking in the mountains and noticing the extraordinary adhesive qualities of burrs that stuck to his clothing.

Metaphor also aids the adoption of an innovation by helping consumers understand and relate to it. The automobile, for instance, was initially described as "a horseless carriage," the motorcycle as "a bicycle with a motor." The snowboard was simply "a skateboard for the snow." The very first step in the evolution that has made the smartphone a ubiquitous and essential device was the launch in 1999 of Research in Motion's BlackBerry 850. It was sold as a pager that could also receive and send emails—a comforting metaphor for initial users.

One needs only to look at the failure of the Segway to see how much harder it is to devise a compelling narrative without a good metaphor. The machine, developed by superstar inventor Dean Kamen and hyped as the next big thing, was financed by hundreds of millions in venture capital. Although it's a brilliant application of advanced technology, hardly anyone uses it.

Many rationalizations can be made for its failure—the high price point, the regulatory restrictions—but I would argue that a key reason is that the Segway is analogous with absolutely nothing at all. It is a little wheeled platform on which you stand upright and largely motionless while moving forward. People couldn't relate to it. You don't sit, as you do in a car, or pedal, as you do on a bicycle, or steer it with handles, as you do a motorcycle. Think of the last time you saw a Segway in use. You probably thought the rider looked laughably geeky on the contraption. Our minds don't take to the Segway because there is no positive experience to compare it to. We're not saying that an Aristotelian argument can't be made without a metaphor; it is just much harder. A horseless carriage is easier to sell than the Segway.

Making Your Choice

When you're facing decisions in the realm of possibilities, it's useful to come up with three or four compelling narratives, each with a strong metaphor, and then put them through a testing process that will help you reach consensus around which one is best. What does that entail?

In the *cannot* world, testing involves accessing and carefully analyzing data. Sometimes that involves simply looking it up—from a table in the Bureau of Labor Statistics database, for example. Other times, it means engaging in an effort to uncover it—such as through a survey. You may also have to apply accepted statistical tests to determine whether the data gathered demonstrates that the proposition—say, that consumers prefer longer product life to greater product functionality—is true or false.

But in the *can* world, where we are seeking to bring something into existence, there is no data to analyze, which means that you have to create data through experimenting with prototypes. You have to create the data by prototyping—giving users something they haven't seen before and observing and recording their reactions. If users don't respond as you expected, you plumb for insights into how the prototype could be improved. And then repeat the process until your prototype is generating data demonstrating that it will work.

Of course, some prototyped ideas are just plain bad. That's why it's important to nurture multiple narratives. If you develop a clear view of what would have to be true for each and conduct prototyping exercises for all of them, consensus will emerge about which narrative is most compelling in action. And involvement in the process will help the team get ready to assume responsibility for putting the chosen narrative into effect.

• • •

The fact that scientific analysis of data has made the world a better place does not mean that it should drive every business decision. When we face a context in which things cannot be other than they are, we can and should use the scientific method to understand that immutable world faster and more thoroughly than any of our competitors. In this context the development of more-sophisticated data analytics and the enthusiasm for big data are unalloyed assets.

But when we use science in contexts in which things can be other than they are, we inadvertently convince ourselves that change isn't possible. And that will leave the field open to others who invent something better—and we will watch in disbelief, assuming it's an anomaly that will go away. Only when it is too late will we realize that the insurgent has demonstrated to our former customers that things indeed can be different. That is the price of applying analytics to the entire business world rather than just to the appropriate part of it.

This chapter is adapted from Roger L. Martin and Tony Golsby-Smith, "Management Is Much More Than a Science," *Harvard Business Review*, September–October 2017.

PART THREE

Structuring Work

6

Culture

You can only change it by altering how individuals work with one another.

T he role and importance of a company's culture is best captured by a combination of two of the world's greatest management scholars. Peter Drucker opined that "culture—no matter how defined—is singularly persistent." (It is an urban myth that he ever said, "Culture eats strategy for breakfast.") MIT Sloan professor Edgar Schein declared that "culture determines and limits strategy." The implication is, of course, that any strategy not predicated on a company's existing culture will fail—unless the culture can be changed, which is challenging in the extreme.

So, what is culture—and why is it so persistent and limiting to strategy?

There are as many definitions of culture as there are for strategy, but I think of it primarily as a book of rules residing in the minds of employees that guides how they interpret situations and decisions. Culture is what helps a manager understand "how things get done around here," "what I should do in this situation," and "who must I pay attention to." The rules making up the culture are developed by each person's observations of how people around them react to and explain situations and decisions, particularly those involving extreme outcomes with significant impact for the people involved, even if such decisions or events are unusual.

The strength of a company's culture is determined by the similarity of the mental rule books of the employees. A culture is weak or diffuse if the rule books vary across people—so that employees' interpretations of a given situation or decision are heterogeneous. Cultures are powerful when the people all have a very similar rule book and consequently interpret and react to the same decision or situation in the same way.

When a new strategy calls for a change in behaviors and values, a powerful culture gets in the way of those changes because all employees will instinctively continue to be guided by their inner rule book in responding to decisions and situations. For example, if a new strategy calls for customizing service but the corporate culture calls for imposing a standard service with no exceptions, the customer will receive the standard service.

CEOs recognize that changing strategic direction in any significant way will inevitably involve some culture change. But most of their efforts fail because they haven't properly internalized a key truth about culture: *you can only change it by altering how individuals work with each other.*

In the following pages I'll explain why cultural change can only be brought about by microinterventions to the ways we structure and prepare for face-to-face work, who turns up, and how the conversations are framed. I will describe what these changes look like and show how they can bring about fundamental changes in patterns of working together, which will in turn change the rules on "how things get done around here," "what I should do in this situation," and "who or what must I pay attention to." I'll demonstrate from my own personal experience of leading a culture change in this way just how powerfully small and innocuous microchanges can transform the culture of an organization.

Let's begin by looking at culture's role relative to the other drivers of organizational behavior.

Organizational Steering Mechanisms

My thinking on culture change is anchored in a concept of organizational steering mechanisms that I first discussed in an HBR article, "Changing the Mind of the Corporation," almost thirty years ago. Three categories of steering mechanisms organize and channel the operations and actions of a company:

- Formal. These include the organizational structures, systems, and processes that are designed to help the firm achieve its goals. They are the result of conscious decisions imposed on the people working in the organization. Examples include the company's reporting structure, the compensation system, and the budgeting process.

- Interpersonal. These mechanisms shape and govern the ways in which individuals interact with each other face-to-face. They are a product of people's psychological makeup and vary widely. For example, does this person prefer to discuss conflicts openly or ignore them?

- Cultural. These are the rules, referred to earlier, captured in people's shared mental guidebooks, through which they interpret decisions and situations and determine how to respond to them. While every organization has cultural mechanisms, in most cases they take shape in unplanned ways and are typically not documented.

As figure 6-1 shows, the three sets of mechanisms form an interrelated system. Take, for example, the typical reporting structure of

FIGURE-6-1

Organizational steering mechanisms

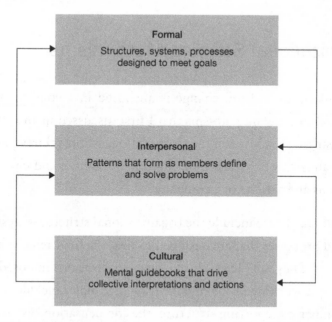

Source: I credit Diana Smith, a fellow student of management thinker and father of the field of organizational learning Chris Argyris, for contributing to my understanding of how the steering mechanisms work as a system as shown in this figure.

independent sales and marketing functions, with each reporting to a separate senior vice president or executive vice president, who in turn reports separately to the CEO or COO. That structure often drives interpersonal conflict (the arrow running from formal to interpersonal) between salespeople and marketers. The salespeople argue that the marketers dream up impractical ideas, and the marketers claim that the salespeople only want to sell the easy stuff. If those conflicts escalate, the organization's leaders may attempt a formal fix (the arrow running from interpersonal to formal), usually through combining the functions into a single marketing and sales function. Hence, formal mechanisms influence interpersonal mechanisms, and interpersonal mechanisms influence formal mechanisms.

The interpersonal conflicts between salespeople and marketers also influence the cultural mechanisms. When a marketer comes to the salespeople with an idea, the rule book says: "Push back hard because marketing is always unrealistic about what can actually be sold." And when new salespeople are brought on board, they are told to be wary of the marketers. That then loops back to the interpersonal domain in which the conversations are likely to be more confrontational still because the culture reinforces that characteristic behavior. Hence, the steering mechanisms work as a system with feedback loops between formal and interpersonal and between interpersonal and cultural. As time passes and the organization grows, the constant feedback between the mechanisms strengthens them, making it increasingly harder for the organization to change.

Any attempt to change an organization, therefore, must involve changes to these steering mechanisms. For CEOs whose strategies require organizational change, the obvious starting point is to change the formal mechanisms—the org chart, incentive systems, and so forth—in part because these are mechanisms that they can easily control but also because a strategic change of direction may require changes to where decision rights and responsibilities are located. And because it can be a struggle for employees to adjust to new formal mechanisms, CEOs recognize that attitudes to these new mechanisms—as determined by the company's culture—must also change to align with the new formal mechanism. And that is where the problems start, because culture cannot be changed directly to align with organizational change.

A Derivative Construct

Somewhat like a neural network in the brain, culture emerges from the interaction between the environment (the formal mechanisms) and individual behaviors (the interpersonal mechanisms). Because of that, little can be done to change the culture of the organization directly by fiat, and CEOs who make the attempt usually lose their jobs. Camillo Pane is a case in point. When he took over as CEO of Coty Inc. in 2016, Pane publicly declared that the struggling fragrance and cosmetics giant needed to begin "acting like a startup" and adopt "a challenger mentality." For all that rhetoric, nothing about Coty's culture or performance changed in the two years following Pane's appointment and he was fired in November 2018.

For a culture to align with changes to the formal mechanisms of the organization, changes are required in the way members of the organization interact. If an organization attempts to merge sales and marketing, for example, that formal change will only increase the interpersonal suspicion between salespeople and marketing unless the norms of their interactions and attitudes—the cultural mechanisms— change to make them more cooperative. Otherwise, the feedback with interpersonal dynamics and the existing cultural norms will combine to render the new organizational structure unworkable, and the company will be forced to abandon its efforts to change.

A classic example is the failed culture change at Nokia. As of the early 2000s, Nokia was the dominant cellphone supplier in the world with more than double the market share of the next highest competitor. But BlackBerry had changed the game with the advent of the smartphone, and Nokia CEO Jorma Ollila knew that his company needed to become more entrepreneurial to prosper in the coming storm as other big players would inevitably enter (and Apple, Google, and Samsung most certainly did). His response was a major restructuring in 2004. He believed that with the right structure and incentives, individual behaviors would change, and a new culture would emerge. What happened instead was that Nokia's people continued behaving and interacting according to the rules they were always used to following, which was rewarded at their local levels, since their immediate bosses shared the same cultural rule book, interpreting and engaging with employees accordingly. A cultural aversion to failure, for example, meant that managers were criticized by their bosses for spending money on experiments that didn't work out, which made them reluctant to take risks, which was hardly conducive to creating a culture of entrepreneurship. By the time this became apparent, the damage was done. As Ollila admits in his own biography, "We knew [in 2004] what was happening, but our mistake was in not being able to turn that into action." Once worth $300 billion, Nokia sold its handheld business to Microsoft for $7.2 billion in 2013, which wrote it off and sold it to former Nokia employees for $350 million in 2016—the price of an inability to change culture for the better.

So, what should CEOs do instead?

How to Change Culture Indirectly

The lesson from experiences like Nokia's is that interpersonal exchanges play a central role in aligning cultural and formal mechanisms. The culture only changes if enough people start behaving differently and the new norm gets internalized. The kinds of changes may seem fairly minor, but something as simple as making everyone at a brainstorming session sit at a round rather than a rectangular table can have a profound impact on people's willingness to speak up, especially the more junior staff who may have more familiarity with competing at the front lines. Let's turn now to look at some specific examples of changes to interpersonal behaviors in which I have been involved.

Structure and preparation: Throwing out the slide deck

When A.G. Lafley became CEO of P&G in 2000, he wanted to shake up the bureaucratic culture that had evolved around the corporate strategy process. The process was anchored on a strategy review of each business by the CEO and the corporate functional heads, and attitudes about this exchange were best summarized by the expression "get in and get out." A meeting was considered successful if business unit presidents going in came out of it with as few changes to their proposals as possible.

In order to achieve that goal, the unit executives came to the meeting armed with a thick and fully "bulletproofed" PowerPoint deck accompanied by dozens of "issue sheets" that they could pull out to provide answers to any question that they could conceivably be asked. A key success metric for the presenting team was that it had an issue sheet prepared for every question that came up—regardless of how many issue sheets needed to be created to ensure that result. It was a gigantic exercise in second-guessing—and the unit teams took weeks to prepare the slide deck and issue sheets. In the meeting, the business unit presidents went through the slide deck in excruciating detail and would respond to questions by drawing at length from the appropriate issue sheet. These meetings sometimes lasted as long as a day.

At A.G.'s request, I carried out a series of interviews with both presenters and reviewers and found that while nobody was even a bit happy with the process, each side imagined that the other found it useful. In an almost textbook example of the Abilene Paradox, in which each member of a family agrees to drive fifty miles for dinner in Abilene, Texas, when in fact each thought they were the only one who had zero interest in going, the reviewers had found the meetings both unpleasant and useless but imagined that the presenters had derived much value from doing all the preparatory work. Meanwhile, the presenters found the reviews unpleasant and useless but imagined that it was a valuable experience for the reviewers.

A.G. and I decided that to change the dynamics of these reviews, we needed to stop people from presenting massive slide decks and issue sheets. For the fall 2001 cycle, we didn't ask for any changes in the materials, timing, or duration of the reviews. We only asked that the deck be sent to us a week before. We would then identify to the team in advance a short list of topics (no more than three) that we wanted to discuss in the review. We specified that no further preparation was required for the discussion and, as we did not want to listen to them presenting a brand-new, lengthy slide deck focused on the discussion points, we insisted that they bring no more than three new pieces of paper to the meeting.

People did their best to thwart us. Some teams begged us to let them present their original decks. Many of them crammed as much as they could in eight-point fonts on the three new pages, offering complete "solutions" for the discussion issues we had set. But we insisted on no presentations and showed zero interest in answers. We just wanted and insisted on robust discussions of the strategy topics that really mattered to the business in question. Each meeting was hard going for A.G. and the corporate team, who had to fight the business unit presidents from leading the discussion back to a comfortable format. But some engaged, and we heard a few things we had not expected.

It took about four years for the business units to fully adjust to the idea that what A.G. really wanted was simply to have a rich strategy discussion that explored ideas—new ways to compete, new growth avenues, fundamental threats—and made sure that the best minds in the company talked together rather than engaged in corporate theater. In due course, unwritten norms and habits around strategy-making changed to fully support a generative thinking exercise that has lasted to this day.

People: Introducing peer working groups

Zurich-based Amcor is the fifth-largest packaging company in the world. Each year it puts a cadre of about a dozen senior executives, typically reporting to a member of the global management team

(GMT), through an executive development program (EDP). For the 2020 cohort, I worked with the Amcor team designing and overseeing the EDP as part of a project to transform the culture surrounding the creation of strategy.

The core element of the EDP is the personal strategic initiative (PSI). Each participant works during the six months of the program on a live strategy question, problem, or issue that they and their GMT bosses agree is important for the participant's business. At the close of the program, they must present the work they have done on their PSIs to their GMT boss with a recommended course of action. The implicit goal of the participant in previous iterations of the program had been to make as perfect a presentation of their PSI as possible. And the approach of most GMT reviewers had been to critique the presentation, as if they were grading the participants. In effect, what should have been an open discussion about strategy had become a performance review.

In order to change the culture of the program, we created four subgroups of three participants who would meet for monthly check-ins in which the stated purpose was that each should help their two peers develop their PSIs. It was a small but powerful change because it enabled participants to present work for discussion that was not yet perfect. Regardless of the quality of their work, the individuals sharing their work would get helpful advice. And the people helping weren't thinking about reviewing and critiquing but rather how to be useful and constructive.

For their final meetings before the EDP review by the GMT executives, we merged the groups down from four to two groups of six so that each participant would get help from three additional colleagues who were new to the work. Once again, the instructions were to provide advice to their colleague on how to make the strategy even better. In the final step, I gave everybody, including the GMT boss, the same explicit instructions—to focus the conversation on how to make the PSI better rather than on assessing how well the participant had done.

It is too soon to be sure that the changes have triggered a fundamental change, but I am optimistic, in part because we just completed the 2021 program to even greater success. Participants and their GMT bosses alike agree that the quality of PSI presentations and work has improved as a result of the additional rounds of peer engagement. They also agree that the discussions are broader in scope and more speculative, which suggests that the PSI exercise does seem to have become less an assessment as a result of the changes to the interpersonal mechanics of the process.

Frames: Asking for help rather than a grade

Relations between the executive team and the board of one venerable *Fortune* 25 company I advised seemed trapped in a downward spiral. The board queried every idea the senior team came up with and expressed its reservations at every piece of good news. The senior team came to meetings on pins and needles, and with every dysfunctional exchange, expectations on both sides fell lower, making the next exchange even worse. Both sides tried some formal fixes: shorter agendas, more time allocated to Q&A, and more comprehensive briefing packs, but nothing worked. The chair appealed to the board members to adopt a more positive culture, but that just made them angry at him.

The root of the problem seemed to lay in an us-versus-them culture, in which (as with the unit presidents at P&G and the EDP participants at Amcor) one side came to sell something to the other side, which felt obligated to grade the performance rather than exchange ideas and insights. The executives would make presentations that were designed to be as perfect and comprehensive as possible and then expect the board to congratulate them on the show. Meanwhile the board members looked rather desperately for ways in which they could be seen to add value to material that they knew relatively little about, which inevitably meant that they ended up looking for contradictions and non sequiturs, consequently coming across as nitpicky.

I advised the executive team to invest less effort in trying to impress the board overall and instead think about getting board members to share insights from their own experience and knowledge. The company was facing a significant technological disruption, so I encouraged the board members to take time to lay out their initial thoughts on how to respond to the disruption in question. Then the CEO asked the board members, "Based on your experiences across a range of industries, what have you seen as the most successful ways of preparing for and navigating through a major disruption of this sort? And what do you think we might be missing in our preliminary approach?"

With this approach, the board members were no longer in the uncomfortable position of passing some kind of judgment on the performance of the executive team on a business they didn't know nearly as well. Instead, they were contributing what they knew a lot about. Several board members had insights from other industries that the executive team found immediately valuable and wouldn't have guessed would serve as useful analogs. Board members engaged in a far more positive way with the executives and reported how impressed they had been with management's thinking. For the executives, who had gone into the meetings with considerable reservations—they had been afraid that they would come across as weak and poorly prepared—seeing the board members react in this way was eye-opening.

Each of the changes I've just described transformed just one part of the rule book in a specific part of the organization—the unit reviews at P&G, the EDP at Amcor, and the board meetings at our *Fortune* 25 company. These were all important local changes that did have major repercussions on the organizations involved, but they were not organizationwide cultural changes. For an example of how small alterations in the preparation, structure, and framing of personal exchanges did transform the overall culture and performance of an organization, I will draw on my own experience of culture change at the University of Toronto's Rotman School of Management, where I served as dean from 1998 to 2013.

Creating a Winning Culture at the Rotman School

When I joined, Rotman had still not recovered from a dispute that had embarrassed the school, forced the previous dean's resignation, and split its faculty into warring camps. Faculty, staff, students, and the outside world alike saw the school as a distant second to the Ivey Business School, then the dominant Canadian business school.

Rotman's culture was toxic. The assumption on the part of faculty and students was that the school and university administrators were not to be trusted and were closed to any change. For their part, administrators saw both faculty and students as irritating and permanently dissatisfied complainers. Both faculty and administration were deeply suspicious of outside stakeholders, including alumni, the Canadian business community, and the Toronto media. I knew that I had to change the rule books in their collective heads in order to have any hope of enabling the school to shine.

As I was a high-profile outside hire from the business community, the assumption was that I would make dramatic changes—that I would reorganize the school and install a "businesslike culture." I didn't. The organizational structure in place when I left in 2013 wasn't much different from that I found on arriving in 1998. The governance structure was identical. There were tweaks, but that was it. I didn't make a bold announcement of a new culture; in fact I didn't talk about culture at all.

Instead, I focused relentlessly on changing the interpersonal steering mechanisms, for example, the way I handled faculty review discussions, faculty conflicts, and meetings with my key staff who worked with outside stakeholders.

Faculty review: How can we help?

When I joined, the system for faculty review imposed on the Rotman School (and every other department) by the University of Toronto required that each faculty member submit an annual activity report to the dean that specified the professor's research, teaching, and service accomplishments in the previous twelve months—that is, books or articles published, invited lectures given, research grants or prizes awarded, courses taught with student evaluations, teaching prizes, committees served on, and so forth. As dean, my task was to issue a standard evaluation letter, informing faculty members of their rankings on a seven-point scale for research, teaching, service, and overall.

I made no changes to that formal mechanism. But I did add one interpersonal interaction: I invited each faculty member to a one-hour meeting with me after they had submitted their report. In that meeting, I asked three questions:

1. To what extent did you meet the goals you set for yourself last year?

2. What are your goals for the upcoming year?

3. In attempting to achieve those goals, do you need some help from the school that you are not now getting?

The reason I added this meeting was to encourage professors to see themselves as in charge of their accomplishments and that my job (and that of the administration) was to help them (within reason) to achieve their intrinsically motivated goals. The conversation wasn't about the dean passing judgment. It was about the dean finding out what they wanted to do and what help they needed to get it done. As dean, I could intervene in administrative processes in order to help faculty members achieve their goals or overcome obstacles, and these meetings uncovered situations where there was a crying need for an intervention.

One case early in my term stands out. Like many business schools, the Rotman faculty consisted of two tracks: research professors on tenure track and nontenured lecturers (later called professors of practice) who were not obliged to do research but taught a higher number of courses per year. Culturally, in most schools, many of the research professors and administrators treat lecturers as second-class citizens. When I asked the third question of a longtime lecturer, Joan, her answer was clear and simple: a laptop computer, which the school administration had refused to provide.

To understand why this was a big deal, you must know that the university has a main downtown campus plus east and west suburban campuses. Joan taught both downtown and at the west campus. Under university rules, all professors or lecturers were given a desktop computer for their office (hers was downtown). Since this was the era before the lecture hall systems were wired into a shared system, Joan had to download her lecture slides from her desktop computer onto floppy disks (remember those?), carry the (right) disks with her to the lecture halls, and then load them onto the lecture hall computers in front of impatient students. All that would be eliminated if Joan could replace her desktop with a laptop that she could carry around with her and plug into any lecture room projector. Despite the eminent good sense of this, the IT administrators insisted each time Joan had approached them that she could not have a laptop because of the university policy.

When I told Joan that she could have her laptop, she asked me whether I was kidding. I assured her that I was deadly serious. When she went to the school's IT department to get a laptop, they phoned me to ask if the policy had changed and that everyone could get a laptop. I responded, "No. But Joan really needs one to do her job." And the decision didn't set a precedent, even though everyone soon found out about it, because everyone understood that I was responding to an individual, customized need, not making a new rule.

My introduction of a conversation framed about helping professors achieve their goals, rather than on how well they had performed, transformed professors' attitudes to the administration. Few faculty members left Rotman during my fifteen years there, and at times when I needed their help (notably in the aftermath of the global financial crisis), they were there for me and the school. Talk about the practice spread—I even got requests from professors in faculties outside the business school asking whether I would be willing to have an annual meeting with them.

Managing conflict: Let's get you both in the room

Among the factors contributing to poor relations between faculty and administration was their perceived role as adjudicator in disputes between academics. Universities are notorious for these conflicts, perhaps, as Henry Kissinger famously quipped, "because the stakes are so small." I quickly found myself receiving visits from faculty members who would come to complain to me about another faculty member in the hope that I would intervene in their favor.

Rather than institute a formal process for conflict resolution or make a general appeal that faculty members resolve their differences directly, I changed the interpersonal dynamic of our meetings, in what I called privately my "campaign for adult behavior." When any faculty member came to my office to complain about a fellow academic, I would cheerily get up from my desk and suggest that the two of us go see the person right away to work it out. That was almost always the opposite of what the complainant wanted, which was to complain to me about someone who annoyed them without the other person being able to push back. Having to watch me hear the other side in their presence might end up making them look foolish.

As I guessed would be the case, no complainant ever took me up on the offer, and within months, people stopped coming to complain to me about colleagues behind their backs. I am not naive enough to think that this behavioral gambit eliminated interpersonal conflict between professors, but it did create a culture in which people worked directly on resolving their conflicts rather than run to the dean. In my last ten years in the role, not a single faculty member complained to me about a colleague.

External stakeholders: Changing the terms of engagement

When I took over as dean, the school had: (1) little interaction with the business community (in the previous year there had been a total of two events in the school to which members of the business community were invited); (2) almost no media profile (reporters called and/ or wrote about our competitors before coming to us); (3) low levels of engagement with alumni (we had active contact information for less than 15 percent of alumni and did almost nothing for them); and (4) a barely visible intellectual profile outside the refereed academic journals (we intermittently produced the *Rotman Magazine*, mailed to the few alumni for whom we had addresses, to little obvious effect). Since we had little financial flexibility to invest net new dollars in any of these external portfolios, I knew I needed to change the attitudes and norms around what we were already doing.

The traditional attitude at the institution had been extractive. We interacted with alumni and business because we wanted to raise money or get our graduates hired. We interacted with the media to get favorable reviews and news stories so that alumni and business would feel good about associating with us. In my meeting with managers in charge of events, media relations, alumni, and the magazine, I pushed to replace this attitude with what I came to call the "Doctrine of Relentless Utility": we would make ourselves as useful to our external stakeholders as we possibly could without asking for anything in return. If we worked hard at doing that, I suggested, good things would happen for the school. Who knows when and who knows how? But something good would result. So, in my conversations with the team members, I would ask them for their ideas on how they could be useful to the stakeholders they engaged with and for ideas on how I and anyone else in the school could help them be useful.

One such idea that continues strongly to this day was to create an annual Lifelong Learning (LLL) day for graduates. The theory of the day was that since new knowledge continues to accumulate after you graduate, we will recall you (like an automobile) to provide you with the knowledge that has accumulated in the following year. And we will do it for you every year so that your school takes responsibility for you being current. We wouldn't charge a penny for it and wouldn't make a fundraising ask, as happens at reunions.

Our LLL day became a huge, popular event that brought us closer to our alumni. It also produced an unexpected response—nonalumni who liked the proposed content so much they wanted to attend. Our first reaction was to not allow nonalums to attend because that would make it less special for our alumni. But then we realized that if we charged nonalumni, we would create more budget room to improve the offering and demonstrate in real dollars the free value that alumni were receiving. Within relatively short order, hundreds of nonalumni were paying $1,000 for a day of LLL, and no alum ever complained.

As conversations along these lines took place and were acted on, attitudes around how Rotman engaged with external stakeholders changed and converged on seeing everything through the lens of relentless utility. As time passed and the fruits of our efforts became apparent, the scale of our engagement increased dramatically. In my last year as dean, we had 122 events attracting over 10,000 people. Our share of media coverage surpassed that of all other Canadian business schools combined, and we were getting at least ten mentions every week in the international press (compared to less than once a month in 1998). We had active addresses for over 90 percent of alumni and high engagement in a variety of alumni events, including LLL. Our magazine appeared on newsstands across Canada and rivaled the *California Management Review* and *MIT Sloan Management Review* in paid circulation. We accomplished all that with a net annual investment (i.e., after event and subscription revenue) that in my final year (2013) was still barely larger than external relations budget I inherited in 1998.

• • •

When executives try to change an organization's culture, they often bring the wrong tools to the task—changes to formal processes and systems along with righteous admonition. This approach is doomed to failure because culture depends not on systems and processes or a leader's beliefs but on how individuals react to each other in the context of their rules and relationships. To achieve real culture change, executives should focus on and show discipline in how they structure the human interactions that make up an organization's working day. That requires investing time and committing to repetition. People won't change their ways overnight, but when they do, the consequences are profound and durable.

This chapter updates and expands on Roger L. Martin, "Changing the Mind of the Corporation," *Harvard Business Review*, November–December 1993.

7

Knowledge Work

You must organize around projects,
not jobs.

ompanies everywhere struggle with the management of
knowledge workers. They compete fiercely to find and retain
the best talent, often accumulating thousands of managers in
the process. For a while this is fine, but inevitably, usually when economic conditions turn less favorable, they realize that these expensive
workers are not as productive as hoped, and in an effort to manage
costs they lay off a large swath of them. Soon after, though, they're
out recruiting again.

This cycle is highly destructive. Aside from the human and social
costs involved, it is extremely inefficient for a company to manage any
resource this way, let alone one that is widely recognized as the engine
of growth in the modern age. What's especially puzzling is that the
companies that engage in this cycle include some of America's most
revered role models. General Electric, for example, conducted extensive management layoffs in the 1980s and early 1990s. After a gradual
regrowth in its ranks, the company announced another round of

layoffs in 2001. By 2007 the numbers were back up again—until the recession forced cuts once more. Colgate-Palmolive, MetLife, Hewlett-Packard, and PepsiCo, among others, have all gone through the same process.

Why do these companies struggle so much with what ought to be their most productive assets? The answer, I think, is rooted in a profound misunderstanding—despite decades of research and debate about the knowledge economy—of how knowledge work does and does not differ from the manual work we have come to understand so well. In particular, most companies make two big mistakes in managing knowledge workers. The first is to think that they should structure this workforce as they do a manual workforce—with each employee doing the same tasks day in and day out. The second (which derives in part from the first) is to assume that knowledge is necessarily bundled with the workers and, unlike manual labor, can't readily be codified and transferred to others.

And this brings me to a different way of thinking about knowledge work: *you must organize around projects, not jobs.* In this chapter I'll demonstrate how destructive, if understandable, traditional assumptions around work are in the context of knowledge work and describe an alternative paradigm. If companies more broadly adopt the model I propose, we may finally be able to bid farewell to the current, perverse hire-and-fire cycle that characterizes most corporations today.

Let's begin by looking at what knowledge workers actually do.

The Rise of the Decision Factory

Knowledge workers don't manufacture products or perform basic services. But they do produce something, and it is perfectly reasonable to characterize their work as the production of decisions: decisions about what to sell, at what price, to whom, with what advertising strategy, through what logistics system, in what location, and with what staffing levels.

At desks and in meeting rooms, every day of their working lives, knowledge workers hammer away in decision factories. Their raw materials are data, either from their own information systems or from outside providers. They produce lots of memos and presentations full of analyses and recommendations. They engage in production processes—called meetings—that convert this work to finished goods in the form of decisions. Or they generate rework: another meeting to reach the decision that wasn't made in the first meeting. And they participate in postproduction services: following up on decisions.

Decision factories have arguably become corporate America's largest cost, even at big manufacturers like P&G, because the salaries of these decision factory workers far exceed those of workers in physical factories. In pursuit of the twin goals of efficiency and growth, companies in the latter half of the twentieth century spent ever-greater amounts on R&D, branding, information technology systems, and automation—all investments that necessitated hiring an army of knowledge workers.

I vividly remember working with the CEO of one of North America's largest bread manufacturers. He had just replaced a labor-intensive and antiquated plant with the most advanced bread bakery on the continent. He proudly told me that the new computerized ovens and packaging machinery had reduced direct labor costs by 60 percent. But meanwhile, a throng of new and expensive knowledge workers had been added at both the head office and the plant—engineers, computer technicians, and managers—to take care of the sophisticated computer systems and state-of-the-art equipment. The new plant wasn't quite the unalloyed good that it appeared at first sight. Variable costs of manual labor fell, but the fixed cost of knowledge workers rose, making it critical to keep capacity utilization high—which was possible in some years but not in others.

The bread company was representative of many businesses. They swapped direct costs for indirect costs, which meant fewer but more productive manual workers and greater numbers of more expensive knowledge workers. (See the sidebar "The Rising Share of Knowledge Work.")

In the half century and more since Peter Drucker coined the term "knowledge workers," these employees have become not just an important part of the workforce but the dominant part. And as China and other low-cost jurisdictions bring more and more manual workers onstream, the developed economies will become ever more reliant on knowledge workers, whose productivity may therefore be *the* management challenge of our times.

Productivity in the Decision Factory

The two critical drivers of productivity in any production process are the way the work is structured and the company's ability to capture the lessons of experience. These drivers are of course interdependent: how you structure the work influences your ability to learn from it. In decision factories, a mismatch between the reality of work and the way it is structured leads directly to inefficiencies in allocating knowledge work. People being people, this mismatch weakens incentives for sharing knowledge. Let's look at why.

Work structure in the decision factory

The basic unit of labor in the decision factory is the job. In this respect, decision factories follow the product factory model, whereby managers typically identify a specific activity that makes up an individual's job and needs to be repeated more or less daily. If you know how much

The Rising Share
of Knowledge Work

One way to get a sense of the magnitude of knowledge workers' rise in the modern workforce is to look at changes in cost of goods sold (COGS) and selling, general, and administrative expenses (SG&A) at large companies. COGS and SG&A spending—by far the largest cost items in any company— serve as a reasonably good proxy for blue-collar and white-collar workers respectively, because the costs of the former are embedded in COGS and those of the latter make up the majority of SG&A.

The Dow Jones 30 (DJ30) has always exemplified American big business: In 2020 its members had revenue of $2.8 trillion and approximately 8 million employees. In 1972, as this graph shows, the DJ30 aggregate spending on COGS was 72 percent of revenue and on SG&A was 13 percent. In the late 1970s, SG&A began to grow as a proportion of revenue. In the following decade, COGS began to fall. By 2020, their relative proportion had shifted dramatically, with COGS down to 52 percent and SG&A up to 20 percent.

Revenue of the Dow Jones 30

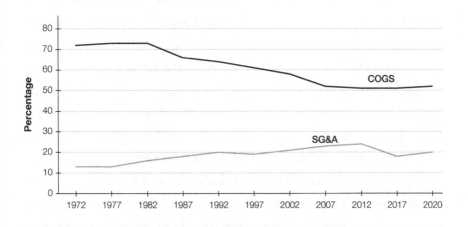

output you want, you can estimate how many of these "jobs" you need and hire accordingly. Of course, output is always somewhat variable, and to the extent that this is predictable, you can build it into job contracts. Some employees work fewer or shorter shifts than others. But on the whole, the assumption implicit in this structure is that the output of product factory work is steady.

Decision factory jobs are based on the same assumption. The vice president of marketing, for example, is implicitly assumed to produce the same amount of output every day. So job descriptions are written as a collection of ongoing tasks that add up to one full-time job. In the prototypical VP of marketing job, the incumbent is responsible for product branding, promotional activities, market research, and so forth—all described as if they needed to be done day after day, week after week, and month after month.

But here the analogy between decision and product factories breaks down. Knowledge work actually comes primarily in the form of projects, not routine daily tasks. Knowledge workers, therefore, experience big swings between peaks and valleys of decision-making intensity. That VP of marketing will be busy during the launch of an important product or when a competitive threat arises—and really, really busy if the two overlap. Between these spells, however, she will have few or even no decisions to make, and she may have little to do but catch up on emails. Yet no one suggests that she vacation during these periods, let alone that the company should stop paying her salary.

Binge-and-purge cycles of hiring and firing knowledge workers are the unfortunate consequence of this approach to knowledge work. When entire workforces are organized around permanent, full-time jobs, it is difficult to redeploy resources to extremely busy areas to deal with peak demand. Typically, the HR department has to create a new position, write a job description, and then fill the position either by transferring someone from another full-time job or by running an external search.

All managers in all areas tend to staff for what they perceive as the peak demand for knowledge work in their area of responsibility. This institutionalizes a significant level of excess capacity spread in small increments throughout decision factories. That is why decision factory productivity is a persistent modern challenge.

Of course, it is most certainly not in the interest of knowledge workers to go to their bosses and declare that they have "spare capacity." At best, they might then be judged in performance reviews as having an easy job and being not very productive. At worst, the bosses might decide that these employees could be cut. Thus it is to every knowledge worker's benefit to look busy all the time. There is always a report to write, a memo to generate, a consultation to run, a new idea to explore. And it is in support of this perceived survival imperative that the second driver of productivity—knowledge transfer—gets perverted.

Knowledge in the decision factory

As I described in my book *The Design of Business*, knowledge development goes through three stages. When a new manufacturing or service operation is created—for example, Intel's first microprocessor chip fabrication facility, in 1983, or Disney's first theme park, in Anaheim, California, in 1955—the task is a *mystery*. What is the optimal process flow through the fabrication plant? How should queues be structured at Disneyland? The pioneering experimental work tends to be inefficient and error-filled, as for any mystery.

In due course, with lots of practice, a body of wisdom is created—what can be called a *heuristic*—that guides how the process is carried out. Intel's next dozen fabrication plants were no longer hit or miss, because knowledgeable masters who had worked on the first one designed them. And as Disney opened its four theme parks at Walt Disney World in Orlando, Florida, it was able to use the Anaheim heuristic.

In product factories, the advancement of knowledge doesn't stop with a heuristic. The culture at large-scale manufacturing and service operations is to keep pushing until the knowledge becomes an *algorithm*—a formula for guaranteed success. An operating manual replaces the knowledgeable master. Less experienced managers can use the algorithm to get the job done. That culture lies behind the success of icons such as McDonald's and FedEx. And the work doesn't stop with the existing algorithm: it is honed and refined in a continuous improvement process.

In the decision factory, however, knowledge tends to remain stubbornly at the heuristic level, where experience and judgment are the key requirements for competent decision-making. A big part of the explanation, of course, is that the knowledge challenge is simply tougher in decision factories. Many decisions have to be made for the first time and are thus in the mystery category. For example, how should a company enter Nigeria, its first developing market? And what about the next country? The proper entry strategy will be different there. Even after making entry decisions for ten countries, the company may not have a heuristic, let alone an algorithm.

But the job-based work structure creates a significant hazard. If experienced knowledge workers turn a skill-based heuristic into an algorithm, they are inviting the company to replace them with lower-skilled, less expensive workers. That is why many organizations find it difficult to get master knowledge workers to spend time teaching apprentices even the heuristics: something else always seems to be more pressing.

Of course, this hazard exists in the blue-collar world as well. But there, knowledge is advanced through the observation of physical processes. From the time of Frederick Winslow Taylor and his infernal stopwatch, blue-collar workers have understood that their work can and will be observed and optimized. The jobs of knowledge workers, however, are hidden between their ears.

Senior executives in modern corporations know that they have more knowledge workers than they need, but they don't know where the excess lies. Thus, when they face a dip in sales or some other tough patch, they reflexively chop knowledge workers, trusting that some portion of the excess will disappear without particularly negative consequences.

There is a better way to run the world's expensive decision factories. It has two central attributes: it adopts the method that successful professional services firms use to manage their human resources, and it embraces the ethic of knowledge advancement found in the best blue-collar factories.

Redefining the Job Contract

The key to breaking the binge-and-purge cycle in knowledge work is to use the project rather than the job as the organizing principle. In this model, full-time employees are seen not as tethered to certain specified functions but as flowing to projects where their capabilities are needed. Companies can cut the numbers of knowledge workers they have on the payroll because they can move the ones they have around. The result is a lot less downtime and make-work.

Think of a freshly hired assistant brand manager for Dove at Unilever. She may initially view her role as pretty standard: helping her boss guide the brand. However, she will quickly learn that the job is ever-changing. This month she may be working on the pricing and positioning of a brand extension. Two months later she may be totally absorbed in managing production glitches that are causing shipment delays on the biggest-selling item in the Dove lineup. Then all is quiet until the boss approaches her desk with yet another project. Within months she will figure out that her job is a series of projects that come and go, sometimes in convenient ways and sometimes not.

Although actually organizing knowledge work around projects may seem a radical idea in mainstream business, it is very familiar to professional services firms, some of which have become as large as manufacturing corporations. In thirty-five years, Accenture has grown from its inception as the "systems integration practice" of Arthur Andersen into an independent firm with revenue similar to Merck's. The iconic consultancy McKinsey & Company would rank around 300th in the *Fortune* 500 if it was a public company.

These companies are made up almost exclusively of knowledge workers. When a project comes in, a team is assembled to carry it out. When the project is finished, the team is disassembled, and its members are put on other projects. They don't have permanent assignments; they have established skill levels that qualify them to work in certain capacities on certain projects.

This ability to channel resources flexibly and seamlessly to projects as they arise enables these consulting firms to do something that their clients cannot—that is, to staff projects that the clients can't handle themselves because the necessary personnel are lodged in permanent assignments. True, for some projects a professional services firm has unique expertise. But often its ability to flow bodies quickly to the task at hand is the reason it was hired. Indeed, professional services firms have grown so quickly in part because they are organized around projects, whereas their clients are organized around permanent jobs.

This approach is not limited to professional services firms. Hollywood studios, for example, have always organized around film projects. A team comes together to plan, shoot, edit, market, and distribute a film. As individual team members finish their tasks, they are assigned to other projects.

A few mainstream corporations have already recognized the power of this model. P&G, for example, was an early adopter. Back in 1998, the company carried out a major operational reorganization. The centerpiece was a shift from four integrated regional profit centers to seven global business units (GBUs)—including baby care, fabric care, and beauty care—along with market development organizations that were responsible for distributing the products of all seven GBUs within their given regions.

A feature of the reorganization was the creation of Global Business Services in order to share information technology and employee services. Shared service organizations had become popular, so the fact that P&G took this step was not in itself notable. But how GBS operated was.

In 2003, under the leadership of Filippo Passerini, who served as the president of GBS until 2015, P&G engaged in what was then the biggest outsourcing deal in corporate history: It sent approximately 3,300 jobs to IBM, HP, and Jones Lang LaSalle. Passerini transferred to those organizations the GBS employees who were performing the most-routine, least-project-oriented work. This allowed him to think more innovatively about the jobs that remained within GBS. The classic move would have been to structure them as flat jobs, assuming a consistent stream of similar work for each one.

Instead Passerini decided to embrace the project nature inherent in the work still at GBS. He made the part of his enterprise that remained within P&G what he called a "flow-to-the-work organization." Of course, some of his employees were still working in flat, permanent jobs, but a large proportion were assigned to whatever projects had high urgency and high payoff. These knowledge workers didn't expect to stay in one business unit in one region; they understood that they would be working in teams organized specifically to tackle pressing assignments in succession.

The integration of Gillette was one such assignment. The 2005 acquisition of Gillette was by far the biggest P&G had ever made, adding 30,000 employees and costing $57 billion. The most challenging aspect lay in the GBS area: integrating all the back-office functions—finance, sales, logistics, manufacturing, marketing—and information technology systems. Thanks to GBS's flow-to-the-work structure, Passerini could quickly channel extensive resources to the integration. As a result, it was accomplished in a mere fifteen months—less than half the time normally required for an acquisition of this size. With synergy savings from integration estimated at $4 million a day, this translated into a saving of close to $2 billion.

The project-based approach to knowledge work is currently being rolled out across P&G. In 2012 the company announced an initiative to eliminate excess white-collar costs and manage the remaining costs more effectively. Each part of the P&G organization is defining what proportion of its knowledge workforce should be in permanent, flat jobs and what proportion should be in flow-to-the-work jobs. The flow proportion may vary by unit, but it is required to be greater than zero.

Toward the Knowledge Algorithm

Switching to a flow-to-the-work structure will do much to improve the productivity of a company's knowledge workers and to remove obstacles to codifying and transferring knowledge. But it will not guarantee that the codification and transfer actually take place.

For that to happen, knowledge workers must be persuaded to go the extra mile. P&G has become a leader in this respect as well, putting key executives in charge of codifying its knowledge. Since 1837 the company has been a model brand builder, but for a long time it left brand building as a heuristic to be developed in the heads of experienced and expensive executives. Learning the heuristic traditionally involved apprenticing with one or more of them to slowly absorb the unwritten rules.

P&G eventually decided that this approach was no longer acceptable. In 1999 Deborah Henretta, then the general manager for fabric conditioners, sponsored a project to codify the company's brand-building heuristic—and thereby move it in the direction of an algorithm. The brand-building framework (dubbed BBF 1.0) was intended to enable young marketers in the organization to learn the techniques for brand building more quickly, thus lowering the time and cost required for this task. BBF was found sufficiently valuable to be further refined, producing a number of BBF update releases, including a refresh in 2021.

GBS has actively moved in the same direction. An example of its efforts involves the labor-intensive preparatory work that finance and accounting (F&A) managers in each of twenty-plus categories across P&G carried out in advance of the annual strategic-planning exercise. Traditionally, a manager would rely on experience to determine what sorts of information would be helpful to the category team in preparing for the strategy work, collect that information from a variety of sources, and organize it in some form.

GBS, whose information systems were tapped to provide much of the data, noticed a pattern of requests for certain kinds of data at a certain time of year by certain kinds of managers. In due course it ascertained that the preparatory materials of all these F&A managers were very similar in content and could easily be assembled by GBS from an algorithm; in fact, most of them could be assembled and spit out by a piece of software that GBS had built. Rather than spend hundreds of hours putting together a data package, each manager could simply email GBS and ask for a preparatory deck for the upcoming strategy process.

Obviously, not all knowledge work can be reduced to algorithms. But with today's machine learning technologies, it's possible to go quite far down that track. In finance and medicine, for example, we are increasingly seeing the application of artificial intelligence to analysis and even decision-making traditionally left to humans. In China, Ant Financial's small-business lending operation makes loan decisions almost entirely through software. The company's algorithms can review a loan applicant's business transactions and communications because it can access the data on Taobao, the e-commerce website of its parent company Alibaba. It can use this data to determine a credit rating in real time, which allows it to process the application within minutes at almost no cost. In medicine, the textbook example is radiography, where machine analysis of scans and X-rays are proving highly accurate at diagnosing patient conditions.

• • •

No organization the size of P&G can become project-based overnight or reduce every heuristic to an algorithm. Nor should it; that would be overkill and very disruptive. But a company with 100 percent flat jobs is almost certainly obsolete. Likewise, knowledge in the modern corporation can be advanced only so fast, and a large share of employees will continue to be invested in running current heuristics. But some people are clearly needed to solve the next new mystery. The key is to invest significant knowledge worker resources in projects that move knowledge forward. Only then can organizations avoid cycles of binge and purge while improving the productivity of their knowledge workers.

This chapter is adapted from Roger L. Martin, "Rethinking the Decision Factory," *Harvard Business Review*, October 2013.

8

Corporate Functions

Give them their own strategies.

"\W/here should we start?" asked Stephen. Recently appointed head of innovation at a large, diversified apparel company, Stephen had been tasked with building a culture of innovation across a pretty traditional, operations-focused set of brands. So, at the end of an innovation workshop, he asked for advice on the smartest place to get started.

The answer? With strategy. Begin by thoughtfully articulating the critical choices facing the innovation function. This would help his team understand where it was headed and how it would get there. He rolled his eyes. "We don't need a strategy for our team," he said. "The brands love us. They know they need us. Creating a strategy would be a waste of time—and we're overwhelmed as it is. In fact, we have more work than we can handle."

And there it was: the very best reason to start with strategy. Stephen's team had more work than it could possibly do. He was trying his best to serve the company and was struggling to keep up. Inevitably, work was falling through the cracks as his team tried to do everything for everyone. By denying that he needed to make strategic choices as the head of a function—about how his team allocated resources, what it prioritized, what it ignored—Stephen was in fact making a choice. He was choosing not to choose. And as a result, his team was failing to achieve much at all.

It's a dynamic I've seen again and again in working with and studying dozens of firms (including some mentioned in this article) across a variety of industries. Most companies accept the notion that corporations and business units need strategies. Leaders might not be great at crafting them—or executing on them—but they do at least recognize the value of clearly articulating how their companies and businesses will win in a particular way. For corporate functions—shared service organizations such as IT, HR, R&D, finance, and so on—the need for strategy is less widely understood. In many firms, functions just exist, serving the company in whatever manner and at whatever scale the business units demand.

This brings me to the *one thing* you need to know about corporate functions, which is this: *they need a strategy too*. And if you don't give them one, they will end up defaulting to one of two unconscious organizational and cultural models, both of which are likely to result in their becoming a drag on corporate performance rather than a driver of it. In this chapter I'll describe the two unconscious strategies, explain why they are damaging to company performance, and present a strategy-making process that will help your functions align with corporate and business strategies.

What Happens If You Don't Choose a Strategy?

There's a secret about strategy that no one tells you: every organization has one, whether or not it is written down and whether or not it is the product of an official strategic-planning process. It can be deduced from the actions the organization takes because, essentially, strategy is the logic that determines what you choose to do and not do in service of a particular goal. The goal may be implicit. It may have evolved over time. The choices may have emerged without discussion and exploration. The actions may be ineffectual in achieving the goal. But the strategy exists nonetheless.

When finance decrees that all investments must have a cash payout within seven years, it is making a strategy choice. It is placing a bet that the relatively immediate benefits from a quick return will outweigh the potential benefits that come from making longer-term investments. When IT decides to outsource application development, it is making a strategy choice. It is betting that lowering costs through outsourcing is a more effective way to create value than building applications internally would be. And when HR chooses to standardize hiring practices around the world, it is making a strategy choice. It is choosing to pursue scale advantages from a shared approach rather than benefits (such as agility and adaptation to local culture) of customizing by region.

Does it really matter if such choices are made without an explicit strategy? I believe it does, because if you choose otherwise, your function will likely default to one of two damaging patterns of behavior.

Doing everything the business units want

I call this the *servile strategy*, and it is predicated on the belief that functions serve at the pleasure of the business units. Or, as one CEO remarked, "Business units do strategy; functions support them." That view feels instinctively right to many managers. A company exists to create products and services for customers, so the business units, which do the creating and serving, rightly drive corporate strategy.

But we should not forget that functions serve customers too: the business units that use their services. Functions that unconsciously adopt the servile strategy try to be all things to all people. As a result, they wind up overworking and underwhelming. They become undifferentiated and reactive, losing their ability to influence the company and access resources. They struggle to recruit and retain talent, because no one wants to work for an ineffectual part of the firm.

A servile corporate function lives under the constant threat of being made redundant. It spreads its resources too widely and thus doesn't serve any business unit particularly well, sometimes prompting units to create their own functional capabilities or to look for a more effective (or at least cheaper) outsourced provider.

Putting the function first

The servile strategy produces some miserable outcomes for people working under it, so it's no wonder that many functional leaders, especially in large organizations, adopt a radically different approach that treats functions and business units as equals in terms of power and importance.

In this *imperial strategy*, leaders put the function's work front and center and pay relatively little attention to how it aligns with the needs of the businesses or the overall strategy of the firm. The IT team creates a center of excellence in machine learning and data analytics—because that's where the action is in IT these days. The risk and compliance team builds a huge apparatus around risk assessment and then looks for ways to insert itself into corporate decision-making wherever it can. The finance team builds sophisticated reporting systems that generate mountains of financial data that may or may not be material to the business units' work.

All imperial function leaders I've met claim that their initiatives are great for the company and its businesses, but they can seldom back up this assertion with any evidence beyond pointing to the example set by companies known for excellence in the function's domain: IT benchmarks Google, finance Goldman Sachs, procurement Walmart, and logistics FedEx. And they emulate those firms irrespective of whether their company's strategy resembles that of the benchmark in any way. Meanwhile, frustrated line managers complain that functions divert corporate resources from the units toward activities that make little difference to the company's competitiveness in the market.

The result, unsurprisingly, is a function that serves itself rather than its customers, much as a monopoly business would. And at some level, such functions are monopolies: business units are often prohibited or strongly discouraged by senior management from using outside vendors for their HR or finance or other services. The trouble is that imperial functions all too easily fall prey to the worst tendencies of traditional monopolies: bloat, arrogance, and overreach. And like most monopolies, they inevitably experience a backlash.

It doesn't have to be like this. Corporate functions can and often do contribute greatly to a company's competitive advantage. Procter & Gamble's products research function, for instance, is critical to helping P&G better understand its customers—a key source of its competitive advantage and a driver of its strategic choices. Similarly, paper and packaging manufacturer WestRock's logistics function plays a central role in driving the innovations in flexible, customized delivery that have given the firm an edge over its competitors.

To follow the lead of these exemplars, functions must eschew unconscious strategies and instead make clear, focused, and explicit choices aimed at strengthening and safeguarding the capabilities that set their company apart in the marketplace.

How to Create Effective Functional Strategy

The first two questions a functional leader should explore when putting together a strategy relate to defining the problem: First, what is the implicit current strategy of the function, as reflected in the choices that it makes every day? And second, what are the strategic priorities of the rest of the corporation, and is the function critical to them?

Asking these questions forces functional leaders to confront what is working about their current strategy and what isn't (whether implicit or explicit). Perhaps there are disconnects between their strategy and that of the company, making the function's choices poorly aligned with organizational needs. In trying to serve all parts of the firm, the function may be underserving those that are key to its success. Or perhaps the function isn't helping the firm develop the right organizational capabilities to deliver on the corporate strategy.

Important though the exercise is as a first step, do not dwell too long on these questions. There is often a temptation to do a great deal of research—documenting what your organization is doing in detail, what functions in competitors are doing, and so on. Exploring ways to solve a problem is far more valuable than obsessing about it. A reasonable expectation is that a group of smart people, using their existing knowledge, should be able to answer the two questions to a good-enough level after a few hours of discussion. For example, it wouldn't take a lot of deep analysis for a car company's executives to determine whether safety and reliability or branding and design were their company's main challenge.

Once consensus has been reached around the status quo, the next step is to consider alternatives to it. This involves answering another pair of interrelated questions.

Where will we play?

For functions, this question is relatively straightforward. Leaders must identify their primary customers inside the firm (which should be the units most important to the firm's overall strategy), the core offering of the function to these customers (which should be closely related to the firm's competitive advantage), and what part of that offering will be outsourced and what part delivered by the function itself.

Let's say that an HR function has identified its main problem as a lack of design creativity across the firm. It might determine that its primary customers are business-unit CEOs, its core value offering is recruiting and developing young designers, and its core internal capability is design talent scouting. It might choose to outsource learning and development to top-flight business and design school partners and rely on outside agencies for administrative recruiting and training.

In determining where to play, different functions may focus on different parts of the corporate strategy. Consider a digital-platform company pursuing aggressive growth in China and Asia. Its HR function should probably focus on that challenge, but its risk and compliance function might focus more on EU regulations, where policy changes could threaten the company's core business.

How will we win?

For corporate or business-unit strategists, determining how to win is relatively straightforward: offer a value proposition to your primary customers that's better than what's offered by companies competing for those customers. General Electric needs to figure out how to provide better value to its business customers than Siemens does; Coca-Cola needs to provide better value to soda drinkers than Pepsi does. In each of these cases, the competitor is easy to identify, and its value proposition and business model can be deduced by observing its products and prices in the marketplace and studying its financial reports.

With functions, the how-to-win question is more challenging. It's not always easy to figure out the relative value to a firm of any given function. Although Verizon can probably do a good job of estimating the value provided by its network function versus T-Mobile's network function, it would most likely have a harder time differentiating between the relative values of the two firms' HR or finance functions. What's more, one company's functions aren't really competing directly with other companies' functions in the same industry. That's because the competing firms may have very different strategies, requiring different capabilities. HR might be hugely valuable for one company, whereas finance is hugely valuable for another. The HR function at the HR-driven company would not want to benchmark HR at the finance-driven company. Functions should compare themselves with functions in other companies only if the companies' strategies are similar. Likewise, it would make no sense for HR and finance to benchmark each other. Often, the appropriate benchmark is an outsourced provider.

To illustrate this kind of strategy-making, let's look at talent management at Four Seasons Hotels and Resorts.

Talent Strategy at Four Seasons

For decades now, the heart of Four Seasons' corporate strategy has been its ability to define luxury as service: to make guests feel welcome, happy, and completely at home. Founder Isadore Sharp, in his 2009 book, points to the company's employees as the driving force of this strategy: "[Our long-term staff] were focused on more than their jobs; they were concerned about guest comfort and their ability to enhance it. And our ability to attract, develop, motivate, and retain such people made our . . . culture a rare advantage."

Indeed, Four Seasons' talent function plays a crucial role in producing its competitive advantage. If we look back at what Sharp and the talent team did through our lens of functional strategy, we can see how they defined their problem and the choices they made to solve it.

Defining the problem

Labor costs in the hotel business, as in most service-based industries, represent a large share of operating expenditures (currently about 50 percent). Accordingly, most hotel chains treat labor as a cost to be minimized. Frontline hotel staffers are treated as replaceable cogs in a massive, fast-moving machine. No wonder, then, that according to the Bureau of Labor Statistics, the 2018 (i.e., pre-Covid-19) annualized employee turnover rate in the industry was 73.8 percent.

Since turnover of frontline employees is so high, most major chains focus their hiring efforts on getting good general managers (who are likely to stay longer) and then building mechanisms to quickly hire lots of new entry-level employees each year. They rarely invest much in frontline retention because it is seen as a lost cause; the huge turn-over rate is treated as an inevitability. Instead they focus on cost-cutting to address labor issues: minimizing staff hours, standardizing to boost productivity, and so on. (See the sidebar "The Territory That Strategy Left Behind.")

When Sharp entered the hospitality business, he saw all these norms in operation. But he slowly began to push back on them. At the time, hotel chains defined luxury largely in terms of space: grand architecture and decor, complemented by highly standardized, obsequious service. Sharp believed that luxury was not just about space but also about how people were treated. And frontline staff would be the key to delivering a new form of service that was warm, welcoming, and capable of filling in for the nurturing support system that guests had left at home and the office.

The standard hotel talent strategy (accepting frontline turnover as inevitable and working to mitigate it; investing in retention and development only for general management staff) would not work with Sharp's new vision for the firm. As the company grew, the talent team needed to make a set of choices that would align with firm strategy and build frontline service capability.

The Territory That Strategy Left Behind

In the first half of the twentieth century, the world's large corporations were almost all organized around functions, including manufacturing, marketing, HR, and finance. But beginning in the late 1950s and continuing through the 1960s, most shifted to a structure organized around product-centered business units, in response to the need for each product line to have a clear strategy and accountability in order to win against competitive products and brands.

As firms grew in scale and scope, it became unwieldy to have the head of manufacturing, the head of marketing, and the head of sales all juggle their particular piece of each product line. A new corporate structure emerged, in which product-line business units developed their own independent functions. Each business unit or product team now performed its own HR work, financial accounting, research and development tasks, and logistics support services, giving rise to the conglomerate form of business organization popular through the 1970s and 1980s.

Determining where to play and how to win

The Four Seasons talent team identified the frontline staff as its internal customer and focused on hiring, retaining, and motivating those employees in ways that set it apart from competitors. Rather than hire by résumé or through third-party recruiters, Sharp committed the necessary resources to put candidates through five interviews—the last with the hotel general manager—before they could be hired. This process produced a more thoroughly vetted cadre of hotel staff, hired for attitude rather than experience.

The talent team also invested in extending staff tenure, making its entry-level jobs the starting point of a career rather than a dead end.

Over time, the pendulum swung back, as it became clear that the conglomerate structure failed to add enough value to the businesses to outweigh the costs of maintaining all those individual functions. Corporations began to recentralize many functional activities, enabling greater specialization, efficiency, and consistency in each area.

These centralized functions were purpose-built to create cost efficiencies or to add value in ways that would not occur if the services were performed in a decentralized and smaller-scale way. Purchasing would be cheaper, global recruiting would be more efficient, and R&D would be more effective at scale, the theory went. Marketing, HR, and finance would be more consistent across the businesses. Unfortunately, through this evolution, the questions of what these functions should (and should not) do and how they should think about strategy were largely left unanswered. The practice of business strategy didn't take shape until the 1960s, when the transition to product-line organizational structures was largely complete.

As a consequence, strategy theory and practice focused entirely on product lines, and the functions were the territory that strategy left behind.

This produced a virtuous circle: if the average tenure at Four Seasons approached twenty years, the talent team could invest ten times the resources per person in hiring, training, and rewards than could competitors, whose employees tended to stay for a year or less. The result for Four Seasons would be far better trained and more experienced hotel employees, without higher talent costs overall.

Under Sharp, Four Seasons enjoyed happier, more loyal, more capable, and longer-serving workers—enabling it to deliver superior service and earn leading-price premiums. It built rigorous systems to ensure that its service capabilities were always present. Its recruiting and hiring system was formalized and scaled. Its training systems became legendary. Four Seasons thrived under Sharp, becoming the largest and most profitable luxury hotel chain in the world. And its talent strategy was a crucial element of this success.

Building Strategies for Supporting Functions

Not all functional strategies are as directly tied to the competitive advantage of a firm as is the talent function at Four Seasons. In cases where the connection is more tenuous, it is still important to understand the choices of the function and the role it plays in helping the company win overall. In the simplest terms, supporting functions need to operate in efficient and cost-effective ways that enable the firm to invest in its sources of competitive advantage. If support functions don't make good choices, they put the overall firm strategy at risk.

Consider a typical risk and compliance function. For some companies, superior risk assessment and mitigation is a source of competitive advantage. But for most, that is not the case, even though the function is essential to keeping the firm in business. For a typical risk function, the strategy problem can be defined in any number of ways. It might be a matter of standards: How do we ensure our compliance training is sufficient to prevent disaster and keep the company out of the news? Or it might revolve around stakeholder issues: How can we help build the company's reputation with investors? Or, How might we help our managers understand and quantify operating risks?

The function also has choices regarding whom to serve and with what offering. For instance, it can choose to serve frontline employees or the business-unit leaders—the CEO or the board of directors. It may see all those groups as potential customers, but it must determine which is the core consumer with whom it seeks to win. A compliance unit that sees the firm's main risks as health and safety issues, for example, might want to focus on managers running factories. It might choose to focus on providing expertise to managers making operating decisions (about factory layout, say, or choice of equipment to be used) or compliance training for workers.

The how-to-win trade-offs are similar. A compliance function supporting decision makers worried about safety could win by forging trusted relationships with those decision makers, going deep rather than broad, so that it comes to be seen as a reliable partner in high-level decision-making. Or it might win by creating individualized online employee compliance training in a high-impact but scale-oriented format, allowing the decision-making manager to increase the frequency of risk-awareness-raising interventions without incurring the significant costs and time involved with conventional training efforts or off-the-shelf training software.

• • •

Functions do not have to be servants to corporate overlords, nor should they be petty tyrants building their own empires. Like their business-unit counterparts, functions can use strategy to guide and align their actions, to more effectively allocate resources, and to dramatically enhance the competitive value they provide. Just like the rest of the company, they make choices every day, and by developing a coherent strategy to guide them, they can become vital engines of the business.

This chapter is adapted from Roger L. Martin and Jennifer Riel, "The One Thing You Need to Know About Managing Functions," *Harvard Business Review*, July–August 2019.

Key Activities

9

Planning

Recognize that it's no substitute
for strategy.

A ll executives know that strategy is important. But almost all
also find it scary because it forces them to confront a future
they can only guess at. Worse, actually choosing a strategy
entails making decisions that explicitly cut off possibilities and options.
An executive may well fear that getting those decisions wrong will
wreck his or her career.

The natural reaction is to make the challenge less daunting by turning
it into a problem that can be solved with tried and tested tools. That
nearly always means spending weeks or even months preparing a comprehensive plan for how the company will invest in existing and new
assets and capabilities in order to achieve a target—an increased share of
the market, say, or a share in some new one. The plan is typically supported with detailed spreadsheets that project costs and revenue quite far
into the future. By the end of the process, everyone feels a lot less scared.

Which is precisely why you need to know a very important truth
about planning: *it is no substitute for strategy*. Planning may be an

excellent way to cope with fear of the unknown, but fear and discomfort are an essential part of strategy-making. In fact, if you are entirely comfortable with your strategic plan, there's a strong chance it isn't very good. You're probably stuck in one or more of the traps I'll discuss in this article. You need to be uncomfortable and apprehensive: true strategy is about placing bets and making hard choices. The objective is not to eliminate risk but to increase the odds of success.

In this worldview, managers accept that good strategy is not the product of hours of careful research and modeling that lead to an inevitable and almost perfect conclusion. Instead, it's the result of a simple and quite rough-and-ready process of thinking through what it would take to achieve what you want and then assessing whether it's realistic to try. If executives adopt this definition, then maybe, just maybe, they can keep strategy where it should be: outside the comfort zone of planning.

Comfort Trap 1: Getting into the Plan

Virtually every time the word *strategy* is used, it is paired with some form of the word *plan*, as in the process of "strategic planning" or the resulting "strategic plan." The subtle slide from strategy to planning occurs because planning is a thoroughly doable and comfortable exercise.

Strategic plans all tend to look pretty much the same. They usually have three major parts. The first is a vision or mission statement that sets out a relatively lofty and aspirational goal. The second is a list of initiatives—such as product launches, geographic expansions, and construction projects—that the organization will carry out in pursuit of the goal. This part of the strategic plan tends to be very organized but also very long. The length of the list is generally constrained only by affordability.

The third element is the conversion of the initiatives into financials. In this way, the plan dovetails nicely with the annual budget. Strategic plans become the budget's descriptive front end, often projecting five years of financials in order to appear "strategic." But management typically commits only to year one; in the context of years two through five, "strategic" actually means "impressionistic."

This exercise arguably makes for more thoughtful and thorough budgets. However, planning must not be confused with strategy. Planning typically isn't explicit about what the organization chooses not to do and why. It does not question assumptions. And its dominant logic is affordability; the plan consists of whichever initiatives fit the company's resources.

Mistaking planning for strategy is a common trap. Even board members, who are supposed to be keeping managers honest about strategy, fall into it. They are, after all, primarily current or former managers, who find it safer to supervise planning than to encourage strategic choice. Moreover, Wall Street is more interested in the short-term goals described in plans than in the long-term goals that are the focus of strategy. Analysts pore over plans primarily to assess whether companies can meet their quarterly goals.

Comfort Trap 2: Focusing on Costs

The focus on planning leads seamlessly to cost-based thinking. Costs lend themselves wonderfully to planning, because by and large they are under the control of the company. For the vast majority of costs, the company plays the role of customer. It decides how many employees to hire, how many square feet of real estate to lease, how many machines to procure, how much advertising to air, and so on. In some cases, a company can, like any customer, decide to stop buying a particular good or service, and so even severance or shutdown costs can be under its control.

Of course, there are exceptions. Government agencies tell companies that they need to remit payroll taxes for each employee and buy a certain amount of compliance services. But the proverbial exceptions prove the rule: costs imposed on the company by others make up a relatively small fraction of the overall cost picture, and most are derivative of company-controlled costs. (Payroll taxes, for instance, are incurred only when the company decides to hire an employee.)

Costs are comfortable because they can be planned for with relative precision. This is an important and useful exercise. Many companies are damaged or destroyed when they let their costs get out of control. The trouble is that planning-oriented managers tend to apply familiar, comfortable cost-side approaches to the revenue side as well, treating revenue planning as virtually identical to cost planning and as an equal component of the overall plan and budget. All too often, the result is painstaking work to build up revenue plans salesperson by salesperson, product by product, channel by channel, region by region.

But when the planned revenue doesn't show up, managers feel confused and even aggrieved. "What more could we have done?" they wonder. "We spent thousands upon thousands of hours planning."

There's a simple reason why revenue planning doesn't have the same desired result as cost planning. For costs, the company makes the decisions. But for revenue, customers are in charge. Except in the rare case of monopolies, customers can decide of their own free will whether to give revenue to the company, to its competitors, or to no one at all. Companies may fool themselves into thinking that revenue is under their control, but because it is neither knowable nor controllable, planning, budgeting, and forecasting it is an impressionistic exercise.

Of course, shorter-term revenue planning is much easier for companies that have long-term contracts with customers. For example, for business information provider Thomson Reuters, the bulk of its revenue each year comes from multiyear subscriptions. The only variable amount in the revenue plan is the difference between new subscription sales and cancellations at the end of existing contracts. Similarly, if a company has long order backlogs, as Boeing does, it will be able to predict revenue more accurately, although the Boeing 737 MAX tribulations demonstrate that even "firm orders" don't automatically translate into future revenue. Over the longer term, all revenue is controlled by the customer.

The bottom line, therefore, is that the predictability of costs is fundamentally different from the predictability of revenue. Planning can't and won't make revenue magically appear, and the effort you spend creating revenue plans is a distraction from the strategist's much harder job: finding ways to acquire and keep customers.

Comfort Trap 3: Self-Referential Strategy Frameworks

This trap is perhaps the most insidious because it can snare even managers who, having successfully avoided the planning and cost traps, are trying to build a real strategy. In identifying and articulating a strategy, most executives adopt one of a number of standard frameworks. Unfortunately, two of the most popular ones can lead the unwary user to design a strategy entirely around what the company can control.

In 1978 Henry Mintzberg published an influential article in *Management Science* that introduced *emergent strategy*, a concept he later popularized for the wider nonacademic business audience in his successful 1994 book, *The Rise and Fall of Strategic Planning*. Mintzberg's insight was simple but indeed powerful. He distinguished between *deliberate strategy*, which is intentional, and emergent strategy, which is not based on an original intention but instead consists of the company's responses to a variety of unanticipated events.

Mintzberg's thinking was informed by his observation that managers overestimate their ability to predict the future and to plan for it in a precise and technocratic way. By drawing a distinction between deliberate and emergent strategy, he wanted to encourage managers to watch carefully for changes in their environment and make course corrections in their deliberate strategy accordingly. In addition, he warned against the dangers of sticking to a fixed strategy in the face of substantial changes in the competitive environment.

All of this is eminently sensible advice that every manager would be wise to follow. However, most managers do not. Instead, most use the idea that a strategy emerges as events unfold as a justification for declaring the future to be so unpredictable and volatile that it doesn't make sense to make strategy choices until the future becomes sufficiently clear. Notice how comforting that interpretation is: no longer is there a need to make angst-ridden decisions about unknowable and uncontrollable things.

A little digging into the logic reveals some dangerous flaws in it. If the future is too unpredictable and volatile to make strategic choices, what would lead a manager to believe that it will become significantly less so? And how would that manager recognize the point when predictability is high enough and volatility is low enough to start making choices? Of course, the premise is untenable: there won't be a time when anyone can be sure that the future is predictable.

Hence, the concept of emergent strategy has simply become a handy excuse for avoiding difficult strategic choices, for replicating as a "fast follower" the choices that appear to be succeeding for others, and for deflecting any criticism for not setting out in a bold direction. Simply following competitors' choices will never produce a unique or valuable advantage. None of this is what Mintzberg intended, but it is a common outcome of his framework, because it plays into managers' comfort zones.

In 1984, six years after Mintzberg's original article introducing emergent strategy, Birger Wernerfelt wrote "A Resource-Based View of the Firm," which put forth another enthusiastically embraced concept in strategy. But it wasn't until 1990, when C.K. Prahalad and Gary Hamel wrote one of the most widely read HBR articles of all time, "The Core Competence of the Corporation," that Wernerfelt's resource-based view (RBV) of the firm was widely popularized with managers.

RBV holds that the key to a firm's competitive advantage is the possession of valuable, rare, inimitable, and nonsubstitutable capabilities.

This concept became extraordinarily appealing to executives, because it seemed to suggest that strategy was the identification and building of "core competencies," or "strategic capabilities." Note that this conveniently falls within the realm of the knowable and controllable. Any company can build a technical sales force or a software development lab or a distribution network and declare it a core competence. Executives can comfortably invest in such capabilities and control the entire experience. Within reason, they can guarantee success.

The problem, of course, is that capabilities themselves don't compel a customer to buy. Only those that produce a superior value equation for a particular set of customers can do that. But customers and context are both unknowable and uncontrollable. Many executives prefer to focus on capabilities that can be built—for certain. And if those don't produce success, capricious customers or irrational competitors can take the blame.

Escaping the Traps

It's easy to identify companies that have fallen into these traps. (See the sidebar "Are You Stuck in the Planning Comfort Zone?") In those companies, boards tend to be highly comfortable with the planners and spend lots of time reviewing and approving their work. Discussion in management and board meetings tends to focus on how to squeeze more profit out of existing revenue rather than how to generate new revenue. The principal metrics concern finance and capabilities; those that deal with customer satisfaction or market share (especially changes in the latter) take the back seat.

How can a company escape those traps? Because the problem is rooted in people's natural aversion to discomfort and fear, the only remedy is to adopt a discipline about strategy-making that reconciles you to experiencing some angst. This involves ensuring that the strategy-making process conforms to three basic rules. Keeping to the

Are You Stuck in the Planning Comfort Zone?

Probably: You have a large corporate strategic planning group.
Probably not: If you have a corporate strategy group, it is tiny.

Probably: In addition to profit, your most important performance metrics are cost- and capabilities-based.
Probably not: In addition to profit, your most important performance metrics are customer satisfaction and market share.

Probably: Strategy is presented to the board by your strategic planning staff.
Probably not: Strategy is presented to the board primarily by line executives.

Probably: Board members insist on proof that the strategy will succeed before approving it.
Probably not: Board members ask for a thorough description of the risks involved in a strategy before approving it.

rules isn't easy—the comfort zone is always alluring—and it won't necessarily result in a successful strategy. But if you can follow them, you will at least be sure that your strategy won't be a bad one.

Rule 1: Keep the strategy statement simple

Focus your energy on the key choices that influence revenue decision makers—that is, customers. They will decide to spend their money with your company if your value proposition is superior to competitors'. Two choices determine success: the where-to-play decision (which specific customers to target) and the how-to-win decision (how to create a compelling value proposition for those customers). If a customer is not in the segment or area where the company chooses to play, she probably won't even become aware of the availability and nature of its offering. If the company does connect with that customer, the how-to-win choice will determine whether she will find the offering's targeted value equation compelling.

If a strategy is about just those two decisions, it won't need to involve the production of long and tedious planning documents. There is no reason why a company's strategy choices can't be summarized in one page with simple words and concepts. Characterizing the key choices as where to play and how to win keeps the discussion grounded and makes it more likely that managers will engage with the strategic challenges the firm faces rather than retreat to their planning comfort zone.

Rule 2: Recognize that strategy is not about perfection

As noted, managers unconsciously feel that strategy should achieve the accuracy and predictive power of cost planning—in other words, it should be nearly perfect. But given that strategy is primarily about revenue rather than cost, perfection is an impossible standard. At its very best, therefore, strategy shortens the odds of a company's bets. Managers must internalize that fact if they are not to be intimidated by the strategy-making process.

For that to happen, boards and regulators need to reinforce rather than undermine the notion that strategy involves a bet. Every time a board asks managers if they are sure about their strategy or regulators make them certify the thoroughness of their strategy decision-making processes, it weakens actual strategy-making. As much as boards and regulators may want the world to be knowable and controllable, that's simply not how it works. Until they accept this, they will get planning instead of strategy—and lots of excuses down the line about why the revenue didn't show up.

Rule 3: Make the logic explicit

The only sure way to improve the hit rate of your strategic choices is to test the logic of your thinking: For your choices to make sense, what do you need to believe about customers, about the evolution of your industry, about competition, about your capabilities? It is critical to write down the answers to those questions because the human mind naturally rewrites history and will declare the world to have unfolded largely as was planned rather than recall how strategic bets were actually made and why. If the logic is recorded and then compared to real events, managers will be able to see quickly when and how the strategy is not producing the desired outcome and will be able to make necessary adjustments—just as Henry Mintzberg envisioned. In addition, by observing with some level of rigor what works and what doesn't, managers will be able to improve their strategy decision-making.

As managers apply these rules, their fear of making strategic choices will diminish. That's good—but only up to a point. If a company is completely comfortable with its choices, it's at risk of missing important changes in its environment. I have argued that planning, cost management, and focusing on capabilities are dangerous traps for the strategy maker. Yet those activities are essential; no company can neglect them. For if it's strategy that compels customers to give the company its revenue, planning, cost control, and capabilities determine whether the revenue can be obtained at a price that is profitable for the company. Human nature being what it is, though, planning and the other activities will always dominate strategy rather than serve it—unless a conscious effort is made to prevent that. If you are comfortable with your company's strategy, chances are you're probably not making that effort.

This chapter is adapted from Roger L. Martin, "The Big Lie of Strategic Planning," *Harvard Business Review*, January–February 2014.

10

Execution

Accept that it's the same thing
as strategy.

The idea that execution is distinct from strategy has become
firmly ensconced in management thinking over the past two
decades. Where the idea comes from is not certain, but in 2002,
in the aftermath of the dot-com bubble, Jamie Dimon, now CEO of
JPMorgan Chase, opined, "I'd rather have a first-rate execution and
second-rate strategy any time than a brilliant idea and mediocre management." In the same year, Larry Bossidy, former AlliedSignal CEO,
coauthored the bestselling book *Execution: The Discipline of Getting
Things Done*, in which the authors declared, "Strategies most often fail
because they aren't well executed."

But the doctrine that execution is the key to a strategy's success is
as flawed as it is popular (and the popularity discourages us from questioning the principle's validity). Let's suppose you had a theory that
heavenly objects revolve around the Earth. Increasingly, you find that
this theory doesn't predict the movement of the stars and planets very
well. Is it more rational to respond by questioning the theory that the

universe revolves around the Earth or to keep positing ever more complicated, convoluted, and improbable explanations for the discrepancy? Applying the Dimon-Bossidy doctrine rather than Occam's razor would have you going in a lot of unnecessary and useless circles.

Unfortunately, this is exactly what often happens when people are trying to understand why their strategy is failing, especially when consulting firms are involved. In fact, the Dimon-Bossidy approach can be a godsend for these firms because it allows them to blame their clients for any mistakes they might make. Firms can in effect say, "It won't be our strategy advice that will let you down but your implementation of that strategy. (To help you get around that problem, we suggest that we do some change management work for you as well.)"

Of course, lining the pockets of consulting firms does nothing to further most companies' performance. The problem is the model that holds that strategy formulation and execution are distinct and different. A more powerful model about execution is: *it's the same thing as strategy*. You cannot talk about execution separately from strategy. As I hope to show in this chapter, the idea that we have to choose between a mediocre, well-executed strategy and a brilliant, poorly executed one is deeply flawed—a narrow, unhelpful concept replete with unintended negative consequences. But the good news is that if we abandon the false distinction between strategy and execution, we can change the outcome.

Misguided by the Metaphor

Most businesspeople think of strategy as the purview of senior managers, who, often aided by outside consultants, formulate it and then hand off its execution to the rest of the organization.

The metaphor that informs our understanding of this process is that of the human body. The brain (top management) thinks and chooses, and the body (the organization) does what the brain tells it to do. Successful action is made up of two distinct elements: formulation in the brain and execution through the body. At the formulation stage, the brain decides, "I will pick up this fork now." Then, at the implementation stage, the hand dutifully picks up the fork. The hand doesn't choose—it *does*. The flow is one-way, from the formulator brain to the implementer hand. That hand becomes a "choiceless doer."

A neuroscientist may quibble with this simplification of the brain and body (and of the true order of operations between them), but it's a fair description of the accepted model of organizational strategy: strategy is choosing; execution is doing.

To make this more concrete, imagine you are the CEO of a large retail bank. You and your team formulate a customer strategy. You flow that strategy down to the bank's branches, where it is executed by the customer service representatives (CSRs) on a day-to-day basis. The CSRs are the choiceless doers. They follow a manual that tells them how to treat the customers, how to process transactions, which products to promote, and how to sell them. The hard work of making all those choices is left to the higher-ups—all the way back up to you. Those on the front lines don't have to choose at all—they just *do*.

Really? Consider an experience I had working with a large retail bank in the early 1980s. The bank was revising its strategy and, as a young consultant, I asked to shadow a teller (what CSRs were called in that era) to get a better sense of the bank's operations. I was assigned to Mary, who was the top teller in her branch. As I observed her over the course of a few weeks, I began to see a pattern in the way Mary dealt with her customers. With some, she was polite, efficient, and professional. With others, she would take a little longer, perhaps suggesting that they transfer some of the extra money in their checking account to a higher-yielding term deposit or explaining new services the bank had introduced. And with some customers she would ask about their children, their vacations, or their health but relatively little about banking and finances. The transactions still got done in these instances of informality but took far longer than the other customer interactions did. Mary seemed to treat each of her customers in one of these three distinct ways.

After a while, I took Mary aside and asked about her approach. "Customers come in three general flavors," she explained. "There are those who don't really like banking. They want to come in, do their deposits or transfers, and get out again painlessly. They want me to be friendly but to manage the transactions as quickly as possible. If I tried to give them financial advice, they would say 'That's not your job.'

"Then there's the second kind of customer, who isn't interested in my being her friend but thinks of me as her personal financial service manager. This customer wants me to be watching her other accounts." She pulled out a drawer and pointed to a set of small file cards. "For those customers, I make up these little files that keep me posted on all of their accounts. This lets me offer them specific advice—because that's what they want from me. If I were to ask about their children or their hip surgery, they'd feel as if I were wasting their time or, worse yet, intruding into their lives.

"Finally, there's a group of people who view a branch visit as an important social event, and they've come in part to visit their favorite teller. If you watch the lineup, you'll see some people actually let others go ahead of them and wait for a specific teller to be available [which happened only with respect to Mary in my observation]. With those folks, I have to do their banking, but I also need to talk to them about their lives. If I don't, it won't be the event that they want, and they'll be disappointed with our service."

Intrigued, I asked Mary to show me in the teller manual where it described this strategic segmentation scheme and the differential service models. Mary went white as a sheet, because of course none of this was in the manual. "It's just something I've tried," she explained. "I want customers to be happy, so I do whatever I can to make that happen."

"But for the middle segment," I pressed, "you have to make these files yourself, cobble something together that bank systems could be designed to provide." (Of course, bank systems did eventually catch up, and banks created sophisticated computerized customer information files that looked a lot like Mary's file cards.) "And frankly," I continued, "other tellers and customers could benefit from your approach. Why don't you talk to your bank manager about the three segments and suggest doing things differently?"

That was too much for Mary. "Why would I ever do that?" she replied, suddenly impatient. "I'm just trying to do my job as best I can. They're not interested in what a teller has to say."

Mary had been set up as a choiceless doer. She had been given a manual that essentially said, "It's all about the transaction—just do the transaction and be friendly." But her own experience and insight told her otherwise. She chose to build and implement her own customer service model, understanding that the ultimate goal of the bank was to create happy customers. To do that, she had to reject her role as a choiceless doer. Rather than obey the teller manual and deliver subpar service, she decided to make choices within her own sphere. She had decided, dare I say, to be strategic.

But Mary understood just as clearly that she was in no position to influence the decisions made at the top of her organization. Although she had chosen to reject the conventional, her superiors had not. So, the bank, which could have benefited from her strategic insights, was shut out. It's a pattern I have seen again and again throughout my career. Often, what senior management needed most—although it was rarely able to recognize it—was to have someone talk with the rank and file in order to understand what was really happening in the business. Senior management couldn't get that information itself because it had created a model in which its employees were convinced that no one was interested in what they had to say.

The Choiceless-Doer Dilemma

The strategy-execution model fails at multiple levels of the organization, not just at the front line. Executives, too, are constrained—by the boards, shareholders, regulators, and countless others that dictate to them. Everyone from the top of the organization all the way down to the very bottom makes choices under constraints and uncertainty. Each time a frontline employee responds to a customer request, he is making a choice about how to represent the corporation—a choice directly related to the fundamental value proposition the company is offering. (See the sidebar "A Warning Unheeded.")

So if we can't draw a line in the organization above which strategy happens and below which execution does, what is the use of the distinction between strategy and execution, between formulation and implementation? The answer is none at all. It is a pointless distinction that in no way helps the organization. In fact, it does great damage to the corporation.

In some cases, employees internalize the choiceless-doer model and stick to it faithfully. The employee follows hard-and-fast rules, seeing only black and white because that is what she has been told to see. Her perception of what her superiors expect drives her behavior. She attempts to achieve faithful execution rather than basing her actions on choices about what would be best for the customer within the broad bounds of the strategy of the corporation. This constrains her choices and turns her into a bureaucrat. Any customer who has ever heard the words, "I'm sorry, there is nothing I can do; it's company policy" or

A Warning Unheeded

Most managers are so used to believing that strategy and execution are distinct from one another that they are blind to whether the strategy-execution approach makes any sense. The notion that strategy and execution are connected isn't new. But apparently we didn't listen carefully enough to the great management theorist Kenneth Andrews, who established the distinction between the formulation of a strategy and its execution in his 1971 book, *The Concept of Corporate Strategy.* He wrote: "Corporate strategy has two equally important aspects, interrelated in life but separated to the extent practicable here in our study of the concept. The first of these is formulation; the second is implementation."

Despite the warning that strategy formulation and implementation or execution are "interrelated in life" and "equally important," four decades later, the strategy-execution theory artificially conceptualizes them as separate. It is high time that we delved a little deeper into the twisted logic of our current approach. If we don't, we are almost certain to fail.

who has called an offshore service call center and listened to the far-away representative read through a script that's utterly unconnected to the problem in front of him knows the pain of dealing with a bureaucrat in a choiceless-doer framework.

Meanwhile, managers, blinded by the rigidness of the strategy-execution model they have come to know, make high-level abstract choices and assume that everything else is simple implementation. They fail to recognize that the choices made at the top will beget a whole array of difficult choices down the line. If employees make sound choices and produce great results, senior management gets (and usually takes) credit for having put in place a great strategy. If, on the other hand, there are poor results (whether due to bad choices by management, by employees, or both), the conclusion will almost certainly be that there was flawed execution. The employees are players in a lose-lose game: little credit if their team wins, lots of blame if their team loses. This bind creates a sense of helplessness, rather than a sense of joint responsibility for success. Inevitably, employees decide simply to punch their timecards rather than reflect on how to make things work better for their corporation and its customers.

It's a vicious circle. Feeling disconnected, employees elect not even to try to share customer data with senior managers. Senior managers then must work around their own organization to get the data necessary to make decisions, typically by hiring outside consultants. Frontline employees find the resulting choices inexplicable and unconvincing because the data comes from outside the organization. The employees feel even more disconnected from the company and more convinced that they are working for idiots as *Dilbert*, the comic strip that lampoons the most pretentious and annoying management behaviors, would say. Senior management blames the frontline employees, frontline employees blame management, and eventually, everyone becomes belligerent. Management imposes executional rules and ways of operating that feel unilateral and arbitrary, and frontline workers act against the spirit of the strategy and withhold data that would aid in decision-making.

In this cold, self-centered world, relationships between levels of the organization do not develop or develop with mistrust. Reflection tends to be limited to what impact those in the rest of the system will have on an individual's ability to succeed; the person does not consider his own possible contribution to the problem. Finally, leadership tends to take too much responsibility for success by planning ever more-complex strategies and ever more-stringent implementation plans, while the middle- and lower-level managers see these efforts, feel helpless, and back off from taking responsibility. These are some of the inevitable costs of the mainstream strategy-versus-execution approach.

Strategy as a Choice Cascade

To fix our problem with strategy failure, we need to stop thinking in terms of the brain-to-body metaphor. Instead, we should conceive of the corporation as a white-water river in which choices cascade from the top to the bottom. Each set of rapids is a point in the corporation where choices could be made, with each upstream choice affecting the choice immediately downstream. Those at the top of the company make the broader, more abstract choices involving larger, long-term investments, whereas the employees toward the bottom make more concrete, day-to-day decisions that directly influence customer service and satisfaction.

At the CEO level, the choice might be as broad as "In what businesses will we participate?" The CEO would consult and consider broadly—within the constraints imposed by his board, investors, company history, resources, and so on—and make a choice.

Let's say the CEO decides that the company will invest heavily in the US retail banking business. Given that decision, the president of that business unit might then ask, "How will we seek to win in US retail banking?" Her choice is still quite broad and abstract, but it is explicitly bound by the choice made above her. She decides that the company will win in the retail banking business through superior customer service. From there, yet more choices follow throughout the organization. The executive vice president (EVP) of branch operations might ask, "What service capabilities must we develop to deliver consistently superior customer service?" If the answer includes ease of interaction for the customer at the branch, the branch manager might ask, "What does that mean for the hiring and training of CSRs and the scheduling of their shifts?" And the rep on a given desk has to ask, "What does all that mean for this customer, right here, right now?"

It can be a very long cascade from the top to the bottom in a large corporation. In the bank example, there would probably be both a regional and an area manager between the EVP and the branch manager. As the cascade grows, its structure and operating principles become more critical. For the decision-making process to work most effectively, each choice must be integrated seamlessly with the others. In this model, employees are encouraged to make thoughtful choices within the context of the decisions made above them. The approach rests on the belief that empowering employees to make choices in their sphere will produce better results, happier customers, and more-satisfied employees.

The choice-cascade model isn't nearly as pervasive as the strategy-execution model, but it is implicitly in use in some of the most successful companies in the world. Let me go back to Four Seasons Hotels and Resorts, one of the world's leading high-end hotel chains and which we discussed in chapter 8. As we saw, chair and CEO Isadore Sharp made the decision early on to build his hotel chain based on a new definition of luxury. He decided, he said, "to redefine luxury as service, a support system to fill in for the one left at home and the office."

The problem, of course, was how to get employees at every level to make choices that realized this desired outcome. Traditionally, hotel employees were poorly paid and considered transient and replaceable. Most hotel chains treated their workers as choiceless doers who were told precisely what to do, when to do it, and how—while watching them like a hawk. But the choiceless-doer model would have been the death of Sharp's vision. He needed every employee, from chambermaid to valet to desk clerk to hotel manager, to make the choices necessary to create a comfortable, welcoming support system for guests. It would have been impossible to make a step-by-step instruction manual of how to create the support system he imagined. So Sharp set out a simple, easy-to-understand context within which his employees could make informed choices. The goal for everyone at Four Seasons would be "to deal with others—partners, customers, coworkers, everyone—as we would want them to deal with us."

The Golden Rule—which Sharp, like most of us, learned as child—proved to be a powerful tool for aligning the cascade of choices at Four Seasons within his chosen context. If a Four Seasons customer had a complaint, every single employee was empowered to make it right in the way that made the most sense to her and treat the guest with the concern and care she herself would like to receive. And Sharp has walked the talk, treating his employees as he would want to be treated, as he wanted his guests to be treated. He has done it, he says, "by paying as much attention to employee complaints as guest complaints, by upgrading employee facilities whenever we upgraded a hotel, by disallowing class distinctions in cafeterias and parking lots, by pushing responsibility down and encouraging self-discipline, by setting performance high and holding people accountable, and most of all adhering to our credo: generating trust."

In short, he did it by letting his people choose. The results have been remarkable. In 2019, Four Seasons appeared on *Fortune*'s list of The 100 Best Companies to Work for the twenty-second consecutive year, one of only eight organizations to appear on the list for every year since the list's inception. The company also ranks first in its category in the J.D. Power and Associates' annual Hotel Guest Satisfaction Index and is routinely honored in the *Condé Nast Traveler* Readers' Choice Awards.

Of course, this empowerment doesn't happen without some encouragement. Leaders like Sharp work hard to create a context in which people below them in the choice cascade understand the choices that have already been made and the rationale for them. Those at the top must also be prepared to engage in discussion—without dominating it—around the downstream choices at each level. This can be made more credible if the leader makes it clear to subordinates that the results from their downstream decisions affect not only themselves but also the upstream decisions on which their choices were predicated (see the sidebar "A Cascade of Better Choices").

A Cascade of Better Choices

Unlike with the strategy-execution approach, in which leaders dictate set strategies and expect subordinates to mechanically follow, the choice-cascade model has senior managers empower workers by allowing them to use their best judgment in the scenarios they encounter. But to effectively enable those individual choices, a choice maker "upstream" must set the context for those downstream. At each level, the choice maker can help his employees make better choices in four specific ways.

1. **Explain the choice that has been made and the rationale for it.** Too often we mistakenly assume that our reasoning is clear to others because it is clear to us. We must take the time to be explicit about the choice we have made and the reasons and assumptions behind that choice, while allowing the opportunity for those downstream to ask questions. Only when the people immediately downstream understand the choice and the rationale behind it will they feel empowered rather than artificially constrained.

2. **Explicitly identify the next downstream choice.** We must articulate what we see as the next choice and engage in a downstream discussion to ensure that the process feels like a joint venture that is informed by a hierarchy. Those upstream must guide and inform those downstream, not leave them to make decisions blindly.

3. **Assist in making the downstream choice as needed.** Part of being a boss is helping subordinates make their choices when they need it. The extent of help required will vary from case to case, but a genuine offer should always be a part of the process.

4. **Commit to revisiting and modifying the choice based on downstream feedback.** We cannot ever know that a given choice is a sound one until the downstream choices are made and results roll in. Hence, the superior has to signal that his choice is truly open to reconsideration and review.

Creating a Virtuous Strategy Cycle

The choice-cascade model has a positive-reinforcement loop inherent within it. Because downstream choices are valued and feedback is encouraged, the framework enables employees to send information back upstream, improving the knowledge base of decision makers higher up and enabling everyone in the organization to make better choices. The employee is now not only the brain but also the arms and legs of the organizational body. He is both a chooser and a doer. Workers are made to feel empowered, and the whole organization wins.

This idea isn't new. Progressive management thinkers have been talking about worker empowerment for decades. But that fact raises an important question: With all that empowerment going on, why do so many people still think that execution is all that matters? One answer could be that the firms those people work for do a terrible job of empowering their employees. But if that were the only problem, they'd just need to empower more and everything would be fixed (in other words, use the same old theory, and just apply it more rigorously). This isn't really empowerment but rather those at the top trying to get workers to buy in to their ideas. As those in charge formulate their strategy, they work with change management consultants to determine how they can generate the buy-in they need. They produce workshops and PowerPoint presentations to persuade those below them to be enthusiastic about the chosen strategy and to execute it mechanically as choiceless doers.

Senior managers who focus solely on winning buy-in from those below them don't tend to ask themselves, "How would I like it if I were on the receiving end?" If they did, they'd probably realize that it seemed detestable. It violates the Four Seasons version of the Golden Rule. Employees don't like the buy-in approach because it creates an artificial distinction between strategy and execution. They are expected to sit there and act as if they enjoy being treated as choiceless doers when they know they have to be something else for this "brilliant" strategy and its attendant buy-in process to be successful. As always, upstream theories, and the decisions based on those theories, constrain downstream experiences. In this case, an upstream theory that divides a company into choosers and choiceless doers turns empowerment into a sham.

It's time to revisit and revise our upstream theory. The business world may be utterly convinced that better execution is the path to greatness, but in truth, a better metaphor would be much more helpful. Only then will the rank-and-file employees of organizations be free of the scourge of buy-in sessions. And only then will the promise of empowerment have a chance of being realized.

This chapter is adapted from Roger L. Martin, "The Execution Trap," *Harvard Business Review*, July–August 2010.

11

Talent

Feeling special is more important
than compensation.

I n the traditional model of business-building, talented and vision-
ary entrepreneurs borrowed capital, hired labor, and purchased raw
materials to create products or services. If their ventures succeeded
and they created more value than it cost them to make the products or
services, they became capitalists themselves, investing (or borrowing
against) the profits they earned in order to expand their businesses.

With the broad expansion of markets in capital in the late nineteenth
century, that model changed. Outside capital became more readily
available to grow businesses, and increasingly the entrepreneurial
model was, in the main, displaced by a model in which professional
managers acted as agents for providers of capital. During much of the
twentieth century, this model was characterized by conflict, as the
managers, who represented the interests of investors, tussled with
unions, which represented labor, over how the value created by a business was to be shared between labor and capital.

In the 1970s, the model evolved further. To begin with, there was
increasing awareness that investors' and managers' interests might

conflict, which provided the underpinning for equity-linked compensation, so as to attempt to align the two parties. At the same time, there was increasing recognition of the importance of managers' know-how and skills in the value creation process, which meant that companies increasingly started competing to hire managers and other specialists, such as scientists and programmers, considered to possess the distinctive talent necessary for success. As a result, over the past four decades, this business talent has been capturing a growing proportion of the value created by the businesses they manage—at the expense of the providers of capital.

What particularly gives business talent a strong hand in the negotiation is the fact that, unlike most of the workforce, it is not seen as fungible, and its work is decidedly not generic. For many jobs in an organization, any number of employees could perform the work, because the work is sufficiently defined and predictable to enable the organization to train multiple employees for it. But the value of work that requires unique talent is dependent on who does the work. A moviemaker could still make a movie with a replacement for Julia Roberts, but it wouldn't be a Julia Roberts movie. The Green Bay Packers could play football without superstar quarterback Aaron Rodgers, but the team would have to run a different offense. If a pharma company loses its star scientist, it would need to change its research program. If a hedge fund loses its investment guru, it would need to change its approach to investing.

As the world has turned into a knowledge economy, people with knowledge and skills have become powerful—whether they are corporate executives, research scientists, financial engineers, money managers, artists, athletes, or celebrities. At the same time, as the capital markets have modernized through innovation and technology, capital has become much easier for firms to get a hold of, which has accelerated the shift in power from capital to talent. And while the earnings power of talent in many domains has skyrocketed over the past forty years, nothing has matched the value extraction power of managerial talent: Steve Ballmer earned the vast majority of his $96 billion fortune for being Bill Gates's first business manager. Eric Schmidt's $19 billion net worth stems from taking Google's reins for a decade; Meg Whitman, $6.4 billion for serving as eBay CEO for ten years.

Unsurprisingly, these eye-popping numbers have given rise to a belief that top-end talent is highly sensitive to and motivated by compensation and that big monetary rewards are key to their recruitment and retention. There is a grain of truth to this. I've certainly met plenty of successful people who are motivated by compensation: CEOs who pump up the perceived value of their company in order to sell it, activist hedge fund managers who destroy companies for short-term gain, investment bankers who get their clients to acquire companies they shouldn't in order to earn big fees, or consultants who sell their clients work that they don't need.

Yet these are not really the people I'm talking about here. None of those me-first people had or has the talent or motivation to make their organizations or teams great for a sustained period. I can say with confidence that in my forty years working with people who really are in the very top category of talent, I haven't met a single truly talented person who is solely or even highly motivated by compensation. And that brings me to an alternative model for thinking about talent: *feeling special is more important than compensation.* As I will show in this chapter, when it comes to managing high-end talent, the secret to success is making people feel like valued individuals, not as members of a group, no matter how elite.

I'll begin with the story of Giles.

Giles's Paternity Leave

Thirty years ago, when I was corunning the strategy consulting boutique Monitor Company, Giles was one of a dozen or so global account managers (GAMs) at the time, and a rising star among them. He approached me to ask for paternity leave for his and his wife's first child, now a fairly standard request but a bit more unusual back then. I readily replied, "Sure, Giles. You're a GAM. At your level, you can do pretty much whatever you want. Take as much time as you need."

He said, "OK," and walked off, looking sullen. I was surprised. He had asked for something, and I had given it to him without quibble or conditions. What was his problem? It finally dawned on me. Giles didn't want to be treated as a member of a class, even if it was the exalted class of Monitor GAMs. There was a dozen of them but only one Giles. He wanted to be treated as an individual. Giles wanted to hear: "We care about you and what you need. If paternity leave is the thing that is particularly important to you, we support you 100 percent."

The result would have been the same—unfettered paternity leave— but the emotional impact was very different. Rather than feeling like just another member of his particular group, he would have felt special, uniquely special.

Since that incident with Giles, I have seen the same dynamic at play again and again. It was because he needed to feel special that basketball icon Michael Jordan famously had his own rules, to the chagrin of some of his teammates. It is why the rock band Van Halen insists that the brown M&Ms be removed from candy bowls in their dressing room. Spoiled brats acting out? I am sure there is some of that. But it's not the major driver.

People like Michael Jordan spend their lives striving to be unique. They perform over and above other people. They prepare more; they work harder. They aspire in ways that court failure. They hold themselves to higher standards. They accept the higher pressure that comes with that territory. And that's why Giles was upset. It was jarring at a very deep level to have worked so hard to be distinct from everyone else and then get treated as just another GAM—even though every year we hired scores of high-end MBAs whose dream it was to one day become a Monitor GAM.

People like Giles aren't just doing a job for you. They create unique outcomes that would no longer be possible if they were to disappear. You can't pigeonhole talented people like Giles into a category and expect to keep them happy. You have to create their own categories for them, even if that means adapting the rest of the organization. If you don't, you and your star will both suffer, as the case of National Football League (NFL) star Aaron Rodgers vividly illustrates.

The Sad Story of Aaron Rodgers

After seventeen years of a stellar career quarterbacking the iconic Green Bay Packers, Aaron Rodgers has established himself as one of the greatest quarterbacks in NFL history, a league in which the quarterback position is unquestionably the most critical to team success. Already he has the fifth-most touchdown passes in history. His career passer rating, the most comprehensive measure of the effectiveness of a quarterback, is the highest in league history for any quarterback with five years or more of starting play. He is a winner, having led the Packers in 2011 to its first Super Bowl win in fourteen years and being named the Super Bowl MVP. He has been named the NFL MVP three times, tied for the second most in league history.

Befitting his elite status, the Packers have twice made Rodgers the highest-paid player in the NFL, first with a five-year extension for $110 million (covering 2015–2019) in 2013 and then in 2018 with a four-year extension for $134 million (covering 2020–2023). Compensation was not an issue: for years, the Packers paid Rodgers as if he was the best player in football. And Rodgers reciprocated by being the superstar face of the franchise.

But at the NFL draft in April 2020, Packers general manager (GM) Brian Gutekunst traded up in the draft to be in a position to pick quarterback prospect Jordan Love, a potential successor to Rodgers, instead of selecting a wide receiver to provide more offensive power for Rodgers. According to all involved, Gutekunst never spoke about his plans with Rodgers in advance. The football press continued to query Rodgers about the shallowness of his wide receiver cadre, especially since the Packers didn't pick a single one in the 2020 draft. In a September 3, 2020, interview, Rodgers expressed enthusiasm for his four top receivers, including Jake Kumerow. On September 4, Gutekunst cut Kumerow, who was immediately picked up by the Buffalo Bills. When asked two months later about the prospects of the Packers picking up a wide receiver at the trade deadline, Rodgers responded, "I truly understand my role. I'm not going to [advocate] for anybody. Last time I [advocated] for a player he ended up going to Buffalo."

Rodgers went on to have an MVP season and led the Packers to the National Football Conference (NFC) championship game at which his coach made the decision to not go for a game-tying touchdown with 2:09 remaining in the game, a decision that sent the Tampa Bay Buccaneers, led by fellow superstar quarterback Tom Brady, to the Super Bowl, which they went on to win.

In late April 2021 stories began to circulate that Rodgers had made the decision not to return to the Packers. Although Rodgers did not confirm it, when pushed during an interview in May, he repeatedly referred to "people issues" in dealing with Packers management. He went on to sit out for the bulk of the normal preseason activities, including most of training camp. He finally reached an agreement with the team to return but only if it subtracted one year from his contractual obligation, enabling him to leave as a free agent after the 2022 season. Shortening a superstar's contract at the height of his career is never something a sports team wants to do.

In a press conference following his return to the team, Rodgers finally opened up about the source of his displeasure:

The organization looks at me and my job as just to play. In my opinion, based on what I have accomplished in this league, the way

I care about my teammates, the way I show up in the locker room, the way I lead, the way I conduct myself in the community, should entitle myself [sic] to a little more input. *The rules are the same for most people, but now and then there are some outliers, guys who have been in an organization for seventeen years, won a few MVPs, where they can be in conversations at a different, higher level* [emphasis added]. I am not asking for anything that other great quarterbacks across the last few decades have not gotten. The opportunity just to be in conversations, so if you are going to cut a guy, based on a meritocracy, who was our second-best receiver in training camp last year for the majority of camp, run it by me. See what I feel. I might be able to change your mind. But at least to be in the conversation makes you feel like you're important; you are respected.

While Rodgers did not mention Tom Brady by name, it is hard to imagine that Brady's 2020 season was not on his mind. After a legendary twenty-year career with the New England Patriots, Brady left for the Tampa Bay Buccaneers, who, unlike the Packers, had not challenged for a title in almost two decades and went on to lead the team to a Super Bowl championship. Along the way, Brady had persuaded the team to trade for his longtime favorite tight end, Rob Gronkowski, who Brady convinced to come out of retirement, and Antonio Brown, a polarizing but supremely talented wide receiver with whom Brady had developed a great rapport during the receiver's short stint with the Patriots.

In contemplating the NFC championship game loss, it is easy to imagine that what made the difference in this close game was that Brady's team gave him his desired offensive weapons, while the Packers declined to bring back Rodgers's second favorite receiver, Randall Cobb, who was playing for Houston in 2020 after not being offered a contract following the 2018 season, his eighth with the Packers. Perhaps it is no surprise that alongside Rodgers's decision to return to practice, the team announced it had signed Cobb for the 2021 season.

But the expectation now is that at the end of the 2021 season or at the very latest the 2022 season, Rodgers will end his relationship with the only NFL team for which he has ever played.

The old guard is pushing back. In 2017 Texans owner Bob McNair courted controversy and player outrage by complaining of "the inmates running the prison" in the modern NFL. In a May 2021 interview, former Packers GM (1991–2000) Ron Wolf referred to the current-day star quarterbacks as "divas" and had this to say: "In my time, they are hired to be, to play the position QB. That's what they are being paid for and that's what they are being paid to do. These guys, they want to pick the coach, pick the players."

To be fair, no allegation has been made that Rodgers asked to pick either the coach or the players. However, he did ask not to be treated as just another player, and the consequences of the Packers' decision to do exactly that—treat him as any other player—will become manifestly clear to them in 2022 at the latest.

The Challenges for Management

Treating stars as special people presents a risk. If all managers who saw themselves as stars wanted a say in every decision, chaos could ensue. So, if you want to run a team of highly talented people, you are going to find ways to make them feel special without putting them in charge. But that's easier than you might think, because feeling special isn't the same as being in charge. In fact, talented people often don't want to be in charge. Let's go back to Giles. He didn't want to be in charge of deciding policy on taking leave. If I had just worded my reply more sensitively to his needs, I would have made him feel special without putting him in charge of anything. He needed to feel that I, representing management, valued him as Giles—not as just another GAM.

As you're thinking about how to make your stars feel special, you could do worse than stick to the following three "never do" rules.

Never dismiss their ideas

Talented people invest huge stores of energy and emotion into developing their skills so that they do well and succeed at the highest level. By
the same token, though, they want to have input into how they apply
those skills and how they develop them. Rodgers's gripe with the Packers was primarily around not being given a voice in decisions that were
key to whether he could lead his team to another Super Bowl victory.

Or take the case of Eric Yuan, who had to overcome eight visa refus-
als before getting a visa to work in the United States. He also had to
overcome his lack of English language skills in order to get a job at
the videoconferencing company Webex. And then he had to perform
in such an outstanding fashion that he helped Webex become the leading videoconference platform and earned himself the position of VP
of engineering for tech giant Cisco Systems after it purchased Webex.
Yuan saw the emergence of smartphone-based videoconferencing as
both a threat to and an opportunity for Webex and in 2010 proposed
that Cisco/Webex rewrite the Webex platform to make it smartphone-
friendly. According to Yuan, the proposal was dismissed by Cisco/
Webex. Less than a year later, Yuan left Cisco/Webex to start up Zoom.
Zoom has gone on to displace Webex as the dominant videoconferencing application, with few giving Webex a chance of reestablish-
ing itself as a legitimate contender.

Do you have to listen to everything top-end talent has to say? Of
course not. That would bring about chaos. But recognize that talent
does not take kindly to being dismissed out of hand. And it always
has options—options that may be damaging or even deadly to you.

Never block their development

Given their investment in the development of their talent, star perform-
ers are extremely sensitive to how their talent is used. If a star feels
that her path forward is blocked and is made to wait for the next

advancement or opportunity, she will take her talent to a place that she feels will not block her path. Deciding when and what opportunities to offer and when to withhold opportunities calls for careful judgment. A star performer will also hold you responsible if he fails because you allowed him to bite off too much. The way to win the loyalty of your stars is to be the provider of opportunities that enable them to keep growing and learning—each in their own individual way—without making success impossible.

Sometimes this means battling the human resources function, which tends to want to treat employees homogenously and limit opportunities to rigid time frames. I recall getting intense pushback from the head of allocations when I wanted to assign a less seasoned consultant to a senior role on a major case. I was told that he wasn't ready and that it wasn't fair to others who were more senior. I offered to look for opportunities on other future cases for those I bypassed on this one and promised to take full responsibility for cleaning up any mess that would derive from giving the senior role to the consultant. Fortunately, it worked out well and catapulted the young consultant into a position that eliminated all such questions about his readiness going forward.

For Eric Yuan, the double whammy of having his idea dismissed and having his path forward blocked ensured that Cisco/Webex would lose his essential talent and create a deadly competitor. In explaining his decision to leave a high-salary, high-status corporate job to create a risky startup, Yuan explained, "I had no choice but to leave to build a new solution from the ground up." If you block talent's progress, you can be sure that it will unblock itself.

Never pass up the chance to praise them

In my experience, a real star rarely, if ever, *asks* for praise—at least not directly. And since top-end talent is highly driven and intrinsically motivated, it's tempting to assume that stars don't need a lot of praise and would be indifferent to pats on the back. It is just the opposite. Talented people spend all their time doing really hard things. To do what they do, they have to flirt regularly with—and actually experience—failure. For this reason, they need recognition. Otherwise, they become resentful or sad and drift away from the organization.

The challenge is spotting when they need that recognition and delivering it in an individualized way—praise that could not be given to anyone other than the recipient. The generic year-end "you've had a terrific year" will be taken negatively, not positively, even if accompanied by a sizable financial reward. You need to tie your recognition to specific accomplishments and acknowledge when your star has evolved.

When I served as dean of the Rotman School of Management, we had many excellent professors, but less than a handful had a disproportionate impact on our global reputation. I always made sure to give them pats on the back for things that I heard they were doing—from a favorable article in the press, to a student comment, to the progress of one of their PhD students.

That was why I had to cringe when a professor friend forwarded me an email response he had received from the dean of his business school. It involved approval for traveling business class. Professors at his school could not fly business class unless given specific onetime approval from their dean. My friend, who was one of the school's brightest stars, had recently undergone major heart surgery and wrote to his dean indicating that his doctor had forbade flying coach class for intercontinental travel. He explained in his email that he needed to travel to an academic conference in Europe to receive a prestigious lifetime achievement award from his academic discipline.

It didn't take a rocket scientist to figure out the subtext to the email: "Hey dean, you probably didn't realize that I had major heart surgery and despite that, I am back on my feet and representing the school. And I have just received the most prestigious award in my field." The dean's response, in its entirety? "Approved." Not: "My goodness. I had no idea about the surgery. I am thrilled you have recovered. And I am so happy for you and proud for the school on this latest accolade in your brilliant career. Of course, you have my approval. And I am going to let media relations know about the award so that they can do a press release on the day of its presentation. Have a great time and thanks again for all you do for the school's reputation."

The subtext of his forwarding the exchange to me was clear as a bell: "I would never ask for praise. But what a cold, uncaring response. I bet you never did that as a dean, Roger." Did the dean in question commit a deadly talent management mistake? I doubt it. But how likely is it that my friend will actively help his dean accomplish the next thing on his to-do list? Not very. How much time would have it taken to craft a useful talent management email? No more than five minutes.

• • •

The requirements for talent management in the modern economy may feel daunting. Talent can extract huge economic sums from the providers of capital and can undermine the capability of the talent-based organization to perform. That said, there is a very positive side to the talent management equation. Talent enables outcomes that would otherwise not be possible—special, tail-of-the-distribution outcomes. And to the extent that you rely on top-end talent to produce outstanding organizational performance, you must treat your best people as individuals: never dismiss their ideas, never allow their progress to be blocked, and never miss the chance to shower them with praise when they succeed.

This chapter expands on Roger L. Martin, "The Real Secret to Retaining Talent," *Harvard Business Review*, March–April 2022.

12

Innovation

The design of the intervention is as
critical as the innovation itself.

Throughout most of history, design was a process applied to physical objects. Raymond Loewy designed trains. Frank Lloyd Wright designed houses. Charles Eames designed furniture. Coco Chanel designed haute couture. Paul Rand designed logos. David Kelley designed products, including (most famously) the mouse for the Apple computer.

As it became clear that smart, effective design was behind the success of many commercial goods, companies began employing it in more and more contexts. High-tech firms that hired designers to work on hardware (to, say, come up with the shape and layout of a smartphone) began asking them to create the look and feel of user-interface software. Then designers were asked to help improve user experiences. Soon firms were treating corporate strategy-making as an exercise in design. Today design is even applied to helping multiple stakeholders and organizations work better as a system.

This is the classic path of intellectual progress. Each design process is more complicated and sophisticated than the one before it. Each was enabled by learning from the preceding stage. Designers could easily turn their minds to graphical user interfaces for software because they had experience designing the hardware on which the applications would run. Having crafted better experiences for computer users, designers could readily take on nondigital experiences, like patients' hospital visits. And once they learned how to redesign the user experience in a single organization, they were more prepared to tackle the holistic experience in a system of organizations.

As design has moved further from the world of products, its tools have been adapted and extended into a distinct new discipline: design thinking. Arguably, Nobel laureate Herbert Simon got the ball rolling with the 1969 classic *The Sciences of the Artificial*, which characterized design not so much as a physical process as a way of thinking. And Richard Buchanan made a seminal advance in his 1992 article "Wicked Problems in Design Thinking," in which he proposed using design to solve extraordinarily persistent and difficult challenges.

But with the increased complexity of the design process, a new hurdle arises: the acceptance of what we might call "the designed artifact"—whether product, user experience, strategy, or complex system—by stakeholders. And this brings me to a key truth about innovation: *The design of the intervention is as critical as the innovation itself.* In this chapter, I'll explain this new challenge and demonstrate how applying design thinking to the processes around innovation can help innovators turn the new worlds they've imagined into realities.

The New Challenge

The launch of a new product that resembles a company's other offerings—say, a hybrid version of an existing car model—is typically seen as a positive thing. It produces new revenue and few perceived downsides for the organization. The new vehicle doesn't cause any meaningful changes to the organization or the way its people work, so the design isn't inherently threatening to anyone's job or to the current power structure.

Of course, introducing something new is always worrisome. The hybrid might fail in the marketplace. That would be costly and embarrassing. It might cause other vehicles in the portfolio to be phased out, producing angst for those who support the older models. Yet the designer usually pays little attention to such concerns. Her job is to create a truly great new car, and the knock-on effects are left to others—people in marketing or HR—to manage.

The more complex and less tangible the designed artifact is, though, the less feasible it is for the designer to ignore its potential ripple effects. The business model itself may even need to be changed. That means the introduction of the new artifact requires design attention as well.

Consider this example: Around 2012, MassMutual was trying to find innovative ways to persuade people younger than forty to buy life insurance—a notoriously hard sell. The standard approach would have been to design a special life insurance product and market it in the conventional way. But MassMutual concluded that this was unlikely to work. Instead, the company worked with IDEO to design a completely new type of customer experience focused more broadly on educating people about long-term financial planning.

Launched in October 2014, "Society of Grownups" was conceived as a "master's program for adulthood." Rather than delivering it purely as an online course, the company made it a multichannel experience, with state-of-the-art digital budgeting and financial-planning tools, offices with classrooms and a library that customers could visit, and a curriculum that included everything from investing in a 401(k) to buying good-value wine. That approach was hugely disruptive to the organization's norms and processes, as it required not only a new brand

and new digital tools but also new ways of working. In fact, every aspect of the organization had to be redesigned for the new service, which is intended to evolve as participants provide MassMutual with fresh insights into their needs.

When it comes to very complex artifacts—say, an entire business ecosystem—the problems of integrating a new design loom larger still. For example, the successful rollout of self-driving vehicles will require automobile manufacturers, technology providers, regulators, city and national governments, service firms, and end users to collaborate in new ways and engage in new behaviors. How will insurers work with manufacturers and users to analyze risk? How will data collected from self-driving cars be shared to manage traffic flows while protecting privacy?

New designs on this scale are intimidating. No wonder many genuinely innovative strategies and systems end up on a shelf somewhere— never acted on in any way. However, if you approach a large-scale change as two simultaneous and parallel challenges—the design of the artifact in question and the design of the intervention that brings it to life—you can increase the chances that it will take hold.

Designing the Intervention

Intervention design grew organically out of the iterative prototyping that was introduced to the design process as a way to better understand and predict customers' reactions to a new artifact. In the traditional approach, product developers began by studying the user and creating a product brief. Then they worked hard to create a fabulous design, which the firm launched in the market. In the design-oriented approach popularized by IDEO, the work to understand users was deeper and more ethnographic than quantitative and statistical.

Initially, that was the significant distinction between the old and new approaches. But IDEO realized that no matter how deep the up-front understanding was, designers wouldn't really be able to predict users' reactions to the final product. So IDEO's designers began to reengage with the users sooner, going to them with a very low-resolution prototype to get early feedback. Then they kept repeating the process in short cycles, steadily improving the product until the user was delighted with it. When IDEO's client actually launched the product, it was an almost guaranteed success—a phenomenon that helped make rapid prototyping a best practice.

Iterative rapid-cycle prototyping didn't just improve the artifact. It turned out to be a highly effective way to obtain the funding and orga-nizational commitment to bring the new artifact to market. A new product, especially a relatively revolutionary one, always involves a consequential bet by the management team giving it the green light.

Often, fear of the unknown kills the new idea. With rapid proto-typing, however, a team can be more confident of market success. This effect turns out to be even more important with complex, intangible designs.

In corporate strategy-making, for example, a traditional approach is to have the strategist—whether in-house or a consultant—define the problem, devise the solution, and present it to the executive in charge. Often that executive has one of the following reactions: (1) This doesn't address the problems I think are critical. (2) These aren't the possibili-ties I would have considered. (3) These aren't the things I would have studied. (4) This isn't an answer that's compelling to me. As a conse-quence, winning commitment to the strategy tends to be the excep-tion rather than the rule, especially when the strategy represents a meaningful deviation from the status quo.

The answer is iterative interaction with the decision maker. This means going to the responsible executive early on and saying, "We think this is the problem we need to solve; to what extent does that match your view?" Soon thereafter the strategy designers go back again and say, "Here are the possibilities we want to explore, given the problem definition we agreed on; to what extent are they the possibilities you imagine? Are we missing some, and are any we're considering nonstarters for you?" Later the designers return one more time to say, "We plan to do these analyses on the possibilities that we've agreed are worth exploring; to what extent are they analyses that you would want done, and are we missing any?"

With this approach, the final step of actually introducing a new strategy is almost a formality. The executive responsible for greenlighting it has helped define the problem, confirm the possibilities, and affirm the analyses. The proposed direction is no longer a jolt from left field. It has gradually won commitment throughout the process of its creation.

When the challenge is introducing change to a system—by, say, establishing a new kind of business or a new kind of school—the interactions have to extend even further, to all the principal stakeholders. We'll now look at an example of this kind of intervention design, which involved a major experiment in social engineering that's taking place in Peru.

Designing a New Peru

Intercorp Group is one of Peru's biggest corporations, controlling almost thirty companies across a wide variety of industries. Its CEO, Carlos Rodríguez-Pastor Jr., inherited the company from his father, a former political exile who, upon his return in 1994, led a consortium that bought one of Peru's largest banks, Banco Internacional del Peru, from the government. Rodríguez-Pastor took control of the bank when his father died, in 1995.

Rodríguez-Pastor wanted to be more than a banker. His ambition was to help transform Peru's economy by building up its middle class. In the newly renamed Interbank he saw an opportunity to both create middle-class jobs and cater to middle-class needs. From the outset, however, he grasped that he couldn't achieve this goal with the "great man" approach to strategy characteristic of the large family-controlled conglomerates that often dominate emerging economies. Reaching it would take the carefully engineered engagement of many stakeholders.

Seeding a culture of innovation

The first task was making the bank competitive. For ideas, Rodríguez-Pastor decided to look to the leading financial marketplace in his hemisphere, the United States. He persuaded an analyst at a US brokerage house to let him join an investor tour of US banks, even though Interbank wasn't one of the broker's clients.

If he wanted to build a business that could trigger social change, absorbing some insights by himself and bringing them home wouldn't be enough, Rodríguez-Pastor realized. If he simply imposed his own ideas, buy-in would depend largely on his authority—not a context conducive to social transformation. He needed his managers to learn how to develop insights too so that they could also spot and seize opportunities for advancing his broader ambition. So he talked the analyst into allowing four of his colleagues to join the tour.

This incident was emblematic of his participative approach to strategy-making, which enabled Rodríguez-Pastor to build a strong, innovative management team that put the bank on a competitive footing and diversified the company into a range of businesses catering to the middle class: supermarkets, department stores, pharmacies, and cinemas. By 2020 Intercorp, the group built around Interbank, employed some 75,000 people and had projected revenues of $5.1 billion.

Over the years, Rodríguez-Pastor has expanded his investment in educating the management team. He sends managers each year to programs at top schools and companies (such as Harvard Business School and IDEO) and has worked with those institutions to develop new programs for Intercorp, tossing out ideas that didn't work and refining ones that did. For example, Intercorp was one of the first companies globally to launch, in conjunction with IDEO, its own design center, La Victoria Lab. Located in an up-and-coming area of Lima, it serves as the core of a growing urban innovation hub.

But Rodríguez-Pastor didn't stop at creating an innovative business group targeting middle-class consumers. The next step in his plan for social transformation involved moving Intercorp outside the traditional business domain.

From wallets to hearts and minds

Good education is critical to a thriving middle class, but Peru was severely lagging in this department. The country's public schools were lamentable, and the private sector was little better at equipping children for a middle-class future. Unless that changed, a positive cycle of productivity and prosperity was unlikely to emerge. Rodríguez-Pastor concluded that Intercorp would have to enter the education business with a value proposition targeted at middle-class parents. (See the sidebar "Intervention Design at Innova.")

Winning social acceptability for this venture was the real challenge—one complicated by the fact that education is always a minefield of vested interests. An intervention design, therefore, would be critical to the schools' success. Rodríguez-Pastor worked closely with IDEO to map one out. They began by priming the stakeholders, who might well balk at the idea of a large business group operating schools for children—a controversial proposition even in a business-friendly country like the United States.

Intervention Design at Innova

Innova Schools launched its initiative to bring affordable education to Peru by holding information sessions on its interactive-learning approach with local parents and students.

Designing a New Model

The team began by exploring the lives and motivations of Innova's many stakeholders to find out how it could create a system that would engage teachers, students, and parents.

Ideas began to crystallize around a technology-enabled model that shifted the teacher from "sage on stage" to "guide on the side" and would make schools affordable and scalable. Teachers tried out software tools and provided feedback on them.

As that strategy solidified, Innova held many sessions with teachers, parents, and school leaders to get feedback on classroom design, discuss ways the schools would evolve, and invite stakeholders into the process of implementation.

Final design guidelines were created for the classroom space, the schedule, teaching methods, and the role of the teacher.

November 2012: Piloting the Program

Full pilots were run in two seventh-grade classrooms in two schools. Teachers were thoroughly trained in the new approach, and the model was repeatedly adapted to address their real-time feedback.

2013–Present: Implementation and Evolution

Today the technology-enabled learning model is being implemented in all twenty-nine of Innova's schools. Innova continues to work with its 940-plus teachers to help them use this new approach. It also regularly runs parent engagement sessions; seeks feedback from teachers, coaches, and students; and iterates on its methodology and curriculum.

Intercorp's first move was starting an award in 2007 for "the teacher who leaves a footprint," given to the best teacher in each of the country's twenty-five regions. It quickly became famous, in part because every teacher who received it also won a car. This established Intercorp's genuine interest in improving education in Peru and helped pave the way for teachers, civil servants, and parents to accept the idea of a chain of schools owned by the company.

Next, in 2010 Intercorp purchased a small school business called San Felipe Neri, managed by entrepreneur Jorge Yzusqui Chessman. With one school in operation and two more in development, Chessman had plans for growth, but Intercorp's experience in building large-scale businesses in Peru could take the venture far beyond what he envisioned. However, the business would have to reengineer its existing model, which required highly skilled teachers, who were in extremely short supply in Peru. Rodríguez-Pastor brought together managers from his other businesses—a marketing expert from his bank, a facilities expert from his supermarket chain, for instance—with IDEO to create a new model, Innova Schools. It would offer excellent education at a price affordable for middle-class families.

The team launched a six-month human-centered design process. It engaged hundreds of students, teachers, parents, and other stakeholders, exploring their needs and motivations, involving them in testing approaches, and soliciting their feedback on classroom layout and interactions. The result was a technology-enabled model that incorporated platforms such as the US online-education pioneer Khan Academy. In it the teacher was positioned as a facilitator rather than the sole lesson provider.

The intervention design challenge was that parents might object to having their children learn via laptops in the classroom, and teachers might rebel at the notion of supporting learning rather than leading it. So after six months of preparation, Innova launched a full-scale pilot and brought in parents and teachers to design and run it.

The pilot demonstrated that students, parents, and teachers loved the model, but some of the assumptions were far off base. Parents didn't object to the teaching approach; in fact, they insisted that the laptops not be taken away at the end of the pilot. Additionally, 85 percent of the students used the laptops outside classroom hours. The model was tweaked on the basis of the insights from the pilot, and both the parents and teachers became huge advocates for the Innova model in nearby locations.

Word of mouth spread, and soon the schools were fully enrolled before they were even built. Because Innova had a reputation for innovation, teachers wanted to work there, even though it paid less than the public system. By 2020, Innova had over sixty schools open serving over 50,000 students.

Spreading the wealth

If it followed conventional business wisdom, Intercorp would have focused on the richer parts of the country's capital, Lima, where a middle class was naturally emerging. But Rodríguez-Pastor recognized that the provinces needed a middle class as well. Fostering one there obviously involved job creation. One way that Intercorp could create jobs was to expand its supermarket chain, which it had purchased from Royal Ahold in 2003 and renamed Supermercados Peruanos.

In 2007 the chain began establishing stores in the provinces. Local consumers were certainly receptive to the idea. When one store opened in Huancayo, curious customers queued up for an hour or more to enter it. For many it was their first experience with modern retail. By 2010 the chain was operating sixty-seven supermarkets in nine regions. Today it boasts 535 stores nationwide.

Early on, Intercorp realized that retail ventures of this kind risked impoverishing local communities rather than enriching them. Though a supermarket did provide well-paid jobs, it could hurt the business of local farmers and producers. Since they were small scale and usually operated with low food-safety standards, it would be tempting to source almost everything from Lima. But the logistics costs of doing that would erode profit margins, and if the chain crowded out the local producers, it might destroy more jobs than it created.

Intercorp thus needed to stimulate local production through early engagement with local businesses. In 2010 the company launched the Perú Pasión program, with support from the Corporación Andina de Fomento (an NGO) and Huancayo's regional government. Perú Pasión helps farmers and small manufacturers upgrade their capabilities enough to supply their local Supermercados Peruano. Over time some of these suppliers have even developed into regional or national suppliers in their own right.

Currently, Supermercados Peruanos sources 220 products from 31 different Perú Pasión suppliers. One is Procesadora de Alimentos Velasquez. Originally a neighborhood bakery serving a few small nearby grocery shops, it began supplying a Supermercados store in 2010, generating just $6,000 in annual sales. Since inception, the bakery has sold over $300,000 in merchandise through Perú Pasión. Concepción Lacteos, a dairy producer, is another success. In 2010 it began supplying its local Supermercados store for about $2,500 in annual sales and since inception has generated nearly $600,000 in Perú Pasión sales. In 2020, Intercorp broadened the program to create an online marketplace for small producers to supply across the entire portfolio of Intercorp companies, and it has already attracted 247 suppliers that generated over $500,000 in sales in the first year.

Intercorp's success in boosting the middle class in Peru depended on the thoughtful design of many artifacts: a leading-edge bank, an innovative school system, and businesses adapted for frontier towns across Peru. But equally important has been the design of the introduction of these new artifacts into the status quo. Rodríguez-Pastor carefully mapped out the steps necessary to engage all the relevant parties in their adoption. He deepened the skills of the executives on his leadership team, increased the design know-how of his people, won over teachers and parents to the idea that a conglomerate could provide education, and partnered with local producers to build their capacity to supply supermarkets. In conjunction with well-designed artifacts, these carefully designed interventions have made the social transformation of Peru a real possibility rather than an idealistic aspiration.

The principles of this approach are clear and consistent. Intervention is a multistep process—consisting of many small steps, not a few big ones. Along the entire journey interactions with the users of a complex artifact are essential to weeding out bad designs and building confidence in the success of good ones.

Design thinking began as a way to improve the process of designing tangible products. But that's not where it will end. The Intercorp story and others like it show that design thinking principles have the potential to be even more powerful when applied to managing the intangible challenges involved in getting people to engage with and adopt innovative new ideas and experiences.

This chapter is adapted from Tim Brown and Roger L. Martin, "Design for Action," *Harvard Business Review*, September 2015.

13

Capital Investment

Assume that its value is reset as soon as it is embedded.

I n 2013 Ellen Kullman, then the CEO of the chemicals giant DuPont and under pressure from shareholders to improve results, decided to sell the company's performance coatings business, a low-growth, low-profit part of the portfolio. Carlyle Group, a private equity firm, paid $1.35 billion to gain full ownership of the business and renamed it Axalta. Carlyle immediately embarked on a major overhaul of the unit, which involved fairly aggressive investment, especially in developing markets.

A mere twenty-one months later, Axalta was doing so well that Carlyle took it public and recouped almost its entire investment by selling just 22 percent of the company. By 2016, three and a half years after the acquisition, Carlyle sold its remaining stake, realizing a total of $5.8 billion on its initial investment.

This is a familiar story, and one that has given PE investors like Carlyle, KKR, and Blackstone a reputation as farsighted management geniuses that can unlock hidden value in the most unpromising assets through a combination of rigorous management, good governance, careful cost control, and, above all, freedom from the short-term results required by investors in the public markets.

Small surprise, therefore, that investors, ever on the lookout to boost their returns, are ramping up holdings in PE funds. The public markets are increasingly seen as a mug's game. And with a flood of capital pouring in, PE firms have moved from buying undervalued business units to buying whole companies whose shareholders are unhappy with management's performance.

Yet celebrated PE turnarounds are usually led by managers with long track records in large public corporations, and the exits take place in a relatively near-term five to seven years. Cost cutting is hardly rocket science, and most of the management practices and strategic tools that PE firms apply—such as design thinking and Six Sigma—are well known and widely taught. Given all that, why are large public corporations like DuPont so willing to off-load lucrative opportunities to private investors?

The answer is rooted in the way many—though not, of course, all—corporations value their businesses and projects. The basic mistake many corporate managers have made (and, the data suggests, continue to make) is to compare estimates of future cash flow with the amount of cash put into the business. Although that sounds perfectly reasonable, it anchors performance measurement in a historical number that very quickly loses relevance.

And this brings me to something you need to know about capital investment: *its value is reset as soon as it is embedded.* As I'll explain in this chapter, once an investment has been made in an asset, the company's expectations for the value it will create are, in effect, publicized. So, if a listed company like DuPont makes a large investment in, say, its coatings unit—perhaps to build a manufacturing plant or to enter a new market—those expectations are immediately factored into the share price. If the unit beats expectations, the perceived value of the investment will increase, resulting in a higher share price. If it simply meets expectations, the value won't budge, and the share price (absent other factors) will remain unchanged. But if the unit falls short of expectations, the market will reduce DuPont's share price, even if the investment continues to generate returns on the cash put in—because those returns were not as high as expected.

What this means is that when measuring the performance of their investments, corporations should consider not the cash put in but the current value of the asset or capability they've invested in, which includes the value that the market already believes the company will create or destroy with that asset or capability.

As we'll see, the failure of corporate managers to recognize this explains why PE firms like Carlyle continue to make huge profits from the businesses they buy from the likes of DuPont. I will begin, however, by comparing the various types of assets that corporations invest in, because the disconnect between the market's perception of investment performance and how the performance is measured is rooted in the nature of the assets involved.

Capital and Its Convertibility

A corporation invests its capital in many types of assets. At one end of the spectrum is what I call *unfettered* capital—cash and its equivalents, such as marketable securities or, indeed, any asset that is tradable and can be swiftly converted into cash. Such assets are typically valued on the balance sheet at their market price, which incorporates all current expectations about the value they will create.

At the other end of the spectrum is *embedded* capital, which has been sunk into an asset that is not readily convertible into cash or its equivalents. It may be a production facility, a distribution network, or a software system. It may also be a brand or a patent. In the absence of available market prices, these assets are assessed on the balance sheet at their purchase value less accumulated charges for depreciation or amortization (calculated according to standard accounting rules). For most corporations, such assets represent the majority of capital investments—they are what enable companies to produce, market, and distribute the products or services they offer, through which value is created.

Typically, companies convert unfettered capital into embedded capital. When a chemical company, for example, builds a polyethylene plant, it is embedding capital it has received from banks or equity investors in an asset that may not be easily sold in exchange for cash. If the polyethylene market heads south—or if the plant turns out to cost more than expected—it can probably be sold only at a big loss. Of course, if the plant was brilliantly built and located, it may be sold for a substantial gain. But either way, it can be sold as a functioning plant only if it has been maintained and is fit for the intended purpose.

That's not as bad as it may sound. Investors and banks give corporate managers capital not to invest in cash and marketable securities but to identify and effectively manage productive assets. As the strategy professor Pankaj Ghemawat has argued in his book *Commitment: The Dynamic of Strategy,* the key to competitive advantage is to make investments that commit the corporation to a particular capability and course of action. If you buy the right assets and capabilities and use them well, they will create value for you in the form of a healthy and sustained cash flow. And the less convertible they are, the more value they will create.

Ghemawat's argument has empirical support. The economists William Baumol, John Panzar, and Robert Willig, in an obscure but important book called *Contestable Markets and the Theory of Industry Structure,* showed that industries in which the key productive assets were reasonably convertible performed worse than industries that featured what the authors called *irreversible assets*. For example, in the US scheduled air transport industry, two of the most expensive assets are planes and gates. It turns out that the market in both planes and gates is very liquid, which means that when an entrant invests capital in the industry, it can extract that capital relatively quickly. The trouble is that when the industry is doing well, companies tend to overinvest, because the cost of commitment is relatively low. Thus, the industry suffers from systematic overcapacity. In this environment, it is hard for a company to create value consistently and sustainably.

Ultimately, corporate managers are there to invest in assets that are not easily convertible. It is by embedding the unfettered capital they receive from investors that companies create value. But how can we tell objectively whether those managers are doing a good job?

How Companies Measure Value Creation

Kellogg professor Al Rappaport (author of the influential 1986 book *Creating Shareholder Value*) and the consulting firm Stern Stewart were instrumental in developing the standard methodologies for measuring shareholder value creation. Rappaport's shareholder value added, or SVA, and Stern Stewart's economic value added, or EVA, were very similar, and both involved comparing two numbers: the return on capital invested and the average cost of capital, weighted to reflect the proportions of debt and equity financing. For simplicity, I'll use EVA here, because it has become more common.

EVA expresses expected net cash flow as a percentage of the dollar value of the amount the company has raised through borrowing and equity issuance, as reported on its balance sheet. To generate EVA, managers typically apply the capital asset pricing model, the inputs of which are publicly available. If the return on capital invested exceeds the cost of capital, the corporation is creating value. If it is less, value is being destroyed.

To make this concrete, let's look at the venerable US pharmaceutical, medical devices, and consumer products giant Johnson & Johnson. In 2018 it sold $81.6 billion worth of goods and services and earned $15.3 billion in post-tax cash flow. To generate that cash flow, J&J deployed an average of $89.1 billion of capital—made up of outstanding equity and long-term debt, booked as the amounts raised. (It started the year with $90.8 billion and ended with $87.4 billion.) So, J&J made a healthy 17 percent cash-flow return on its capital invested over the year. During the same period, outside organizations estimated J&J's weighted average cost of capital (WACC) at around 6 percent. So, its positive EVA was 11 percentage points. The other way to think about it is in absolute dollar terms. J&J implicitly incurred a capital charge of about $5.3 billion (6 percent of $89.1 billion) and produced a cash flow of $15.3 billion: it had created about $10 billion in value. This is known as residual cash flow (RCF)—that is, the dollar amount generated over and above the capital charge. If the RCF is positive, the corporation created shareholder value; if negative, it destroyed shareholder value.

In due course, EVA practitioners began applying this corporate-level analysis to individual business units to see which were contributing to or diminishing corporate value creation, because the majority of a firm's embedded-capital investment decisions are made within those units. (At J&J only 16 percent of total assets by dollar value are held at the corporate level.) To calculate the capital charge, analysts identify (from the financial report) the book value of the net assets (fixed assets plus net working capital) associated with each unit (adding in, if they want to be more precise, a pro rata share of corporate assets). Multiplying that adjusted number by the firm's average cost of capital gives a dollar value for a year's capital charge for each business unit.

This type of analysis enabled corporate managers to rank their company's units in terms of RCF, from those generating the most absolute shareholder value to those diminishing it to the greatest extent. For example, J&J divides its business into three main units: pharmaceuticals (which features blockbuster drugs such as Remicade and Xarelto and earns about $8.9 billion of the adjusted cash flow while utilizing about 46 percent of the company's $89.1 billion in invested capital at book value); medical devices (such as stents and contact lenses; $4.4 billion and 35 percent respectively); and consumer products (Band-Aids, baby shampoo, Neutrogena, and so forth; $2.0 billion and 19 percent respectively).

Corporate managers quickly adopted this approach as the basis for important investment and divestiture decisions. Shareholder-value-creating businesses justified more investment; shareholder-value-destroying businesses justified austerity—not throwing more good money after bad.

Nothing about this reaction to the new measurement tool was crazy on its face. Why wouldn't one fund businesses that generate cash in excess of capital costs and be very careful with those that don't cover capital costs? Isn't that what shareholders want? Shouldn't one divest losing businesses before they add yet another year of shareholder value destruction?

So why did J&J's share price fall in 2018, leaving it with a market-value loss of $30 billion or so? We can explain away $23 billion as a reflection of a drop in the overall market—but that still implies that the market believed that J&J destroyed more than $7 billion in value instead of creating the $10 billion or more that the standard analysis identified. If we assume that the market is always right, something must be wrong with the calculation I've just dragged you through. This brings me to the counterintuitive thing you need to know about capital.

Realizing Value at the Moment of Investment

A company's stock price reflects the value investors expect its portfolio of projects to generate. Now, let's imagine that J&J surprised the market by announcing that a new blockbuster drug, previously thought to be a long shot, had received regulatory approval, and that the expected annual profits from it were likely to be some $6 billion a year. Let's further imagine that the analysts covering J&J concurred with that estimate. Other things being equal, with a cost of capital of approximately 6 percent, that $6 billion a year in profit would probably cause J&J's market capitalization to rise by $100 billion.

What's more, the J&J stock price wouldn't rise at a rate of $397 million per trading day (252 a year), because that amount is the extra profits J&J would earn each trading day. Rather, the market would take the news, discount all future extra cash flows stemming from the new drug back to the present, and push the market cap up by $100 billion immediately. That is, of course, with perfect information. If the information trickled out slowly and selectively, it might take some time for the $100 billion bump to materialize. But regardless, the bump was foreordained the moment the surprise regulatory approval occurred.

So again, this is the counterintuitive thing you need to know about capital: *any investment in an asset establishes expectations that value will be created or destroyed in the future, which should be immediately reflected in the value of the capital.*

This is precisely why Alphabet trades overall at eight times its book value. Investors have long since revalued upward the capital embedded in the Google search business—a spectacularly profitable business, which traditional calculations would reveal to have a very high EVA. But that alone would not cause Alphabet's stock price to rise.

Investors would bid up the stock only if they discovered that the company had figured out how to generate a positive RCF after making a capital charge that incorporated the value already embedded in the stock price, not the historical investment. The only thing that pushes up a stock price is positive new information.

Now recall how embedded capital is valued: it is booked as the cash paid to acquire the asset, adjusted by depreciation and amortization. It seems perverse that we factor in expectations of future value when we value a firm's whole portfolio, but not when we're estimating the value of that portfolio's assets—and thus of embedded capital—at the individual business unit or project level.

What's more, by not immediately factoring in the value that an investment is expected to help create, the traditional method implicitly assumes that the next dollar invested will produce the same returns the previous dollar did. That is, if the investment already embedded in a business is destroying (or creating) shareholder value, added investment will do likewise. Of course, that may be the case: there is a good chance that winning businesses picked a winning strategy or business model, so doubling down would indeed create yet more shareholder value. And losing businesses may well have chosen a losing strategy, so doubling down would just produce more value destruction.

But history is not destiny, and it is rarely at all clear that an incremental dollar of capital investment in a high RCF on book (that is, as traditionally calculated) business will also create value. It depends entirely on the nature of the project involved. The trouble is—and here's the trap—if the business already earns a high positive book RCF, it will almost certainly continue to do so after the additional investment, because that investment is unlikely to be large in comparison with the cumulated historical investments. So even if the new investment actually *destroys* shareholder value, the overall book RCF will still be high—leading executives to think that investing in the business continues to be a good idea when it really isn't.

Similarly, it is not at all clear that the next dollar of capital investment in a negative book RCF business won't create value. It is quite conceivable that more than anything else, the business needs an injection of capital. However, unless that injection is dramatically successful, the business will probably still earn a negative book RCF overall, because even if the new investment actually creates a lot of shareholder value, it probably can't undo in one go all the sins of past investments—leading executives to think that it's a poor investment when it isn't.

How can we avoid falling into this trap?

A New Approach

The answer lies in how the capital charge is calculated. It should immediately reflect the expectations of value created or destroyed at the time unfettered capital is transformed into embedded capital.

At the company level, this is a fairly straightforward calculation: at any given time, a corporation's expected cash flow divided by the market value of its combined equity and debt yields a metric called *expected cash flow return on market capitalization*. That's the rate of return an investor would expect to get from buying shares at that time.

At the business unit level, the value of embedded capital can be calculated by dividing the unit's cash flow by the corporate parent's cash flow return on market capitalization. The capital values of all the business units will add up to the market cap of the whole corporation. Finance experts may point out that this approach does not properly account for differing levels of systematic risk and differing optimal capital structures among businesses and projects within the corporation, so the weighted average cost of capital for each business, and therefore the capital charge, would require further adjustments. But in general, that's a minor quibble, because most investors default to simply applying the company's overall WACC to each project or business unit.

If the market cap immediately takes into account all available information about value, including the value known by the market to have been created or destroyed, the RCF at the moment of investment should be zero, and the cost of capital is equal to new investors' expected return on capital.

After the investment is made, what creates or destroys the value of capital is new information that causes managers and analysts to revise their expectations about future cash flow; the new consensus causes the share price to change. To return to J&J and the hypothetical good news from the regulator: the capital charge for the business in which the new blockbuster drug was created—say, oncology—should immediately have been increased by $6 billion a year, the amount shareholders started to expect from the business the moment the regulatory news was incorporated into the stock price. New investors buying that capital from current investors by acquiring shares would be paying for the added value. Similarly, if J&J had instead delivered an indication that it was revising its expectations for year-end profits in oncology upward or downward by, say, 10 percent, that information should have led to an adjustment of its capital charge.

Let's now see if using this approach can explain why J&J ended up destroying $7 billion or so rather than creating the $10 billion suggested by the basic EVA calculations. As noted above, J&J's businesses generated a cash flow of $15.3 billion in 2018. Data in the annual report indicated that it used $89.1 billion of capital to produce those returns.

The Common Mistake in Calculating Value Creation

Most companies use return on invested capital (ROIC) to evaluate how a business is performing. But calculating ROIC requires accurately estimating the firm's cost of capital—and many managers do that incorrectly, by focusing on the book value (or historical cost) of the investment rather than the market value of that capital today (based on the company's stock price). Consider the example from Johnson & Johnson shown in figure 13-1 to understand the pitfalls of that approach.

However, at the end of 2017 the market value of J&J's long-term debt and equity amounted to $405.5 billion—about $316 billion above book value. That is the value that the $89.1 billion cash investment had created or was expected to create as of the end of 2017, according to everything investors then knew about the assets, management's plans, and J&J's business environment. Anyone wanting to invest in J&J at that time would have to pay for the added value then embedded, as reflected in the price. That means that investors who bought J&J shares on January 1, 2018, would be looking at the expected annual return on $405.5 billion, not on the $89.1 billion on the books; otherwise, they wouldn't have invested at the $405.5 billion valuation. The return on the next dollar of investment is what would be relevant to them, and they would be expecting that return to be, at a minimum, the company's WACC of 6 percent. So, what did they get?

By typical measures, J&J had a terrific year in 2018. Sales were up almost 7 percent. After-tax return on book capital was 17 percent against the cost of capital of 6 percent. But the return on market capitalization of the cash flows was, as the figure shows, far less impressive, coming in at 3.8 percent—more than two percentage points below

FIGURE 13-1

Alternative J&J valuations

AVERAGE BOOK VALUE APPROACH

*Most management teams use the **average book value** of capital when assessing returns. Even after subtracting its cost of capital (6%), J&J's businesses appear to be performing well. (All figures are in billions.)*

Business unit	Average book value of capital	2018 cash flow total (% return)	Cost of capital (6% of average book value)	Real cash flow
Pharma	$40.8	$8.9 (21.8%)	– $2.4	= $6.5
Devices	$31.1	$4.4 (14.1%)	– $1.9	= $2.5
Consumer	$17.2	$2.0 (11.6%)	– $1.0	= $1.0

For example, on J&J's books, the company has invested $40.8 billion in its pharma business . . .   . . . which would give it $6.5 billion in real cash flow after adjusting for the cost of capital.

MARKET VALUE APPROACH

*But if we make the same calculations using the **market value** of the capital J&J has invested in each business instead, the results are very different. In fact, J&J's businesses are generating negative cash flow after its real cost of capital is correctly incorporated, which helps explain J&J's lackluster stock performance during this period.*

Business unit	Market value of capital	2018 cash flow total (% return)	Cost of capital (6% of market value)	Real cash flow
Pharma	$236.5	$8.9 (3.8%)	– $14.2	= –$5.3
Devices	$115.1	$4.4 (3.8%)	– $6.9	= –$2.5
Consumer	$53.9	$2.0 (3.7%)	– $3.2	= –$1.2

But the market value approach shows that investors consider $236.5 billion to be their investment in pharma . . .   . . . which makes its real cash flow negative.

J&J's cost of capital. That represents a destruction of shareholder value amounting to $9 billion (just above 2 percent of $405.5 billion) over the year, which would more than account for J&J's notional $7 billion share of the $30 billion loss in the market value of its capital. In fact, as the figure shows, none of J&J's three businesses earned a return on its cost of market capital.

• • •

The idea that the value of capital should always incorporate current expectations may help explain why PE firms do so well. Large corporations that evaluate business performance on a traditional EVA basis probably look to divest themselves of what they see as businesses that offer few prospects for value creation and are thus undeserving of time or money. What PE firms see is an arbitrage opportunity to purchase capital at a price that captures the corporation's artificially low expectations. If companies could truly appreciate that capital markets deal in expectations rather than historical fact, and make investment decisions accordingly, PE firms would probably lose one of their biggest sources of profit.

This chapter is adapted from Roger L. Martin, "What Managers Get Wrong about Capital," *Harvard Business Review*, May–June 2020.

14

M&A

You need to give value to get value.

n 2015, less than a decade after a global financial crisis, the business world set a record for mergers and acquisitions. The value of deals eclipsed the previous record, set in 2007, which had surpassed an earlier peak in 1999. And the party is still in full swing, despite a global pandemic and political turmoil in the United States and Europe. Volume increased in 2016 over 2015, and 2017 over 2016. Six of the seven top years all-time for M&A activity were 2015–2020.

One of the manifestations of the M&A frenzy is the emergence of the special-purchase acquisition company, or SPAC, which first appeared in the 1990s but lay largely dormant until recently with fewer than twenty SPAC initial public offerings per year through 2016. Their creation exploded to 248 SPAC IPOs in 2020 and 435 through the first three quarters of 2021. These companies raise capital without any existing business in operation and only the promise that they will acquire something.

The boom seems impervious to the accelerating pattern of giant failures. We all thought that Microsoft's 2015 write-off of 96 percent of the value of the handset business it had acquired from Nokia for

$7.9 billion the previous year was bad. Or, Google unloading for $2.9 billion the handset business it bought from Motorola for $12.5 billion in 2012; or HP's write-down of $8.8 billion of its $11.1 billion Autonomy acquisition; or News Corporation's 2011 sale of Myspace for a mere $35 million after acquiring it for $580 million just six years earlier; or Yahoo's sale of Tumblr for a reported $3 million in 2019, a mere six years after paying $1.1 billion for it, a 99.7 percent write-off.

But these paled in comparison to the M&A disasters of 2021. Mere months apart in February and May 2021, AT&T spun off its DirecTV subsidiary for consideration of $16 billion and its Time Warner subsidiary for $43 billion, respectively. Spinning off businesses is not inherently a bad thing—in fact, many praised AT&T for getting rid of things that absolutely didn't belong in its portfolio. However, the spin-offs take on a different feel when considered in the context of the purchase prices: $48 billion for DirecTV in 2015 and $85 billion for Time Warner in 2018. That is $74 billion in shareholder capital flushed down the proverbial toilet in under six years. Unsurprisingly, shareholders called for and got the head of the CEO who made the deals, Randall Stephenson, who was retired in 2021.

To be sure, we've seen successes. The purchase of NeXT in 1997 for what now looks like a trivial $404 million saved Apple and set the stage for the greatest accumulation of shareholder value in corporate history. The purchase of Android for $50 million in 2005 gave Google the biggest presence in smartphone operating systems, one of the world's most important product markets. And Warren Buffett's rolling acquisition of GEICO from 1951 to 1996 created Berkshire Hathaway's cornerstone asset. And while it is early to tell, the 2020 Charles Schwab acquisition of TD Ameritrade does appear to be heading in the right direction. But these are the exceptions that prove the rule confirmed by nearly all studies: M&A is a mug's game, in which typically 70 percent to 90 percent of acquisitions are abysmal failures.

Why is the track record so bad? The surprisingly simple answer is the counterintuitive thing you need to know about M&A: *you need to give value to get value.* Companies that focus on what they are going to get from an acquisition are less likely to succeed than those that focus on what they have to give it. (This insight echoes one from Adam Grant, who notes in his book *Give and Take* that people who focus more on giving than on taking in the interpersonal realm do better, in the end, than those who focus on maximizing their own position.)

For example, when a company uses an acquisition to enter an attractive market, it's generally in "take" mode. That was the case in all the disasters just cited. AT&T wanted to get into satellite TV distribution and content creation and delivery. Microsoft and Google wanted to get into smartphone hardware, HP wanted to get into enterprise search and data analytics, and News Corporation wanted to get into social networking. When a buyer is in take mode, the seller can elevate its price to extract all the cumulative future value from the transaction—especially if another potential buyer is in the equation. AT&T, Microsoft, Google, HP, News Corporation, and Yahoo paid top dollar for their acquisitions, which in itself would have made it hard to earn a return on capital. But in addition, none of them understood their new markets, which contributed to the ultimate failure of those deals, because that meant they brought nothing to their acquisitions.

But if you do have something that will render an acquired company more competitive, the picture changes. As long as the acquisition can't make that enhancement on its own or—ideally—with any other acquirer, you, rather than the seller, will earn the rewards that flow from the enhancement. An acquirer can improve its target's competitiveness in four ways: by being a smarter provider of growth capital; by providing better managerial oversight; by transferring valuable skills; and by sharing valuable capabilities. Let's look at each in more detail.

Be a Smarter Provider of Growth Capital

Creating value by being a better investor works well in countries with less developed capital markets and is part of the great success of Indian conglomerates such as Tata Group and Mahindra Group. They acquire (or start up) smaller companies and fund their growth in a way that the Indian capital markets don't.

It's harder to provide capital this way in countries with advanced capital markets. In the United States, for example, activists often force diversified companies to break up because the companies' corporate banking activities can no longer be shown to add competitive value to their constituent businesses. Big companies such as ITT, Motorola, and Fortune Brands, and smaller ones such as Timken and Manitowoc, have been broken up for this reason. Even GE has slimmed down dramatically. One of the biggest deals of 2015 was the proposed $68 billion merger and subsequent three-way split of DuPont and Dow, which resulted from relentless activist pressure on DuPont. More recently, the 2020 announcement of IBM's intention to split into two businesses by the end of 2021 was greeted favorably.

But even in developed countries, being a better investor gives scope for creating value. In new, fast-growing industries, which experience considerable competitive uncertainty, investors that understand their domain can bring a lot of value. In the virtual reality space, for example, app developers were confident that Oculus would be a successful new platform after Facebook acquired it, in 2014, because they were certain that Facebook would provide the requisite resources. So, they developed apps for it, which in turn increased the platform's chances of success.

Another way to provide capital smartly is to facilitate the roll-up of a fragmented industry in the pursuit of scale economies. This is a favorite tool of private equity firms, which have earned billions using it. In such cases, the smarter provider of capital is usually the biggest existing player in the industry, because it brings the most scale to each acquisition (until returns on scale max out). Of course, not all fragmented industries have the potential to deliver scale or scope economies—a lesson learned the hard way by the Loewen Group (Alderwoods after bankruptcy). Loewen rolled up the funeral home business to become the biggest North American player by far, but its size alone created no meaningful competitive advantage over local or regional competitors.

Scale economies aren't necessarily rooted in operating efficiencies. Often they arise through the accumulation of market power. After eliminating competitors, the big players can charge higher prices for value delivered. If this is their strategy, however, they inevitably end up playing cat and mouse with antitrust regulators, who sometimes prevail—as they did in the intended mergers of GE and Honeywell, Comcast and Time Warner, AT&T and T-Mobile, and DirecTV and Dish Network.

Provide Better Managerial Oversight

The second way to enhance an acquisition's competitiveness is to provide it with better strategic direction, organization, and process disciplines. This, too, may be easier said than done.

Super successful, high-end, Europe-based Daimler-Benz thought it could bring much better general management to modestly successful, midmarket, US-based Chrysler and learned a painful $36 billion lesson. Similarly, GE Capital was certain it could bring better management to the many financial services companies it bought in the process of ramping up from a small sideline into GE's biggest unit. As long as the US financial services sector was growing dramatically relative to the nation's economy overall, it appeared that GE was right—the company's approach to management was superior and value-adding for those acquisitions. But when that sector-wide party came crashing to a halt during the global financial crisis, GE Capital nearly brought the whole group to its knees. Perhaps GE Capital improved operations of the acquired companies somewhat, but any improvements paled in comparison to the huge increase in risk that GE Capital took on.

Berkshire Hathaway has a long track record of buying companies and boosting their performance through its management oversight, but Warren Buffett has publicly admitted that it overpaid substantially for its part of the Kraft Heinz deal that it did in collaboration with Brazilian PE firm, 3G Capital.

US conglomerate Danaher may offer the best example of adding value through management. Since its inception, in 1984, it has made more than 400 acquisitions and has grown to a $27 billion company with a market capitalization above $230 billion as of late 2021. Observers as well as Danaher executives attribute its nearly unbroken record of success to the Danaher Business System, which revolves around what the company calls "the four P's: people, plan, process, and performance" and is installed, run, and monitored in every business without exception. For the system to be successful, Danaher asserts, it must improve competitive advantage in the acquired company, not just enhance financial control and organization. And it must be followed through on, not just talked about.

Transfer Valuable Skills

An acquirer can also materially improve the performance of an acquisition by transferring a specific—often functional—skill, asset, or capability to it directly, possibly through the redeployment of specific personnel. The skill should be critical to competitive advantage and more highly developed in the acquirer than in the acquisition.

A historical example is Pepsi-Cola's transfer to Frito-Lay, after the two merged in 1965, of the skills for running a direct store delivery (DSD) logistics system—a key to competitive success in the snack category. A number of PepsiCo DSD managers were assigned to head up Frito-Lay's operations. PepsiCo's 2000 acquisition of Quaker Oats was less fulfilling, however, because the majority of Quaker's sales involved the traditional warehouse delivery method, in which PepsiCo had no skill advantage over Quaker.

Google's purchase of Android provides a modern example of successful transfer. As one of the world's greatest software companies, Google could turbocharge Android's development and help turn it into the dominant smartphone operating system—but it fell short with the hardware-centric Motorola handset business, where Google had no special advantage.

Clearly, this method of adding value requires that the acquisition be closer to home than not. If the acquirer doesn't know the new business intimately, it may believe that its skills are valuable when they aren't. And even when they are valuable, it may be hard to transfer them effectively, especially if the acquired company isn't welcoming toward them.

Share Valuable Capabilities

The fourth way is for the acquirer to share, rather than transfer, a capability or an asset. Here the acquiring company doesn't move personnel or reassign assets; it merely makes them available.

Procter & Gamble shares its multifunctional, colocated customer team capability and its media buying capability with acquisitions. The latter may lower the advertising costs of even large acquisitions by 30 percent or more. With some acquisitions, it also shares a powerful brand—for example, Crest for the SpinBrush and Glide dental floss.

(That approach didn't work for P&G's 1982 acquisition of Norwich Eaton Pharmaceuticals, whose distribution channel and product promotion differed from P&G's.)

Microsoft shared its powerful ability to sell the Office suite to PC buyers by including Visio software in Office after it acquired the company in 2000 for close to $1.4 billion. But it had no valuable capability to share when it bought the handset business from Nokia.

In this form of "give," success lies in understanding the underlying strategic dynamics and ensuring that the sharing actually happens. In what is hailed as the greatest M&A bust of all time—the merger of AOL and Time Warner for $164 billion in 2001—vague arguments were made for how Time Warner could share its content capability with the internet service provider. But the economics of sharing didn't make sense. Content creation is a highly scale-sensitive business, and the wider a piece of content's distribution, the better the economics for its creator. If Time Warner had shared its content exclusively with AOL, which then owned approximately 30 percent of the ISP market, it would have helped AOL competitively but damaged itself by shutting off the other 70 percent. And even if Time Warner had limited itself to giving AOL preferential treatment, the other market players might well have retaliated by boycotting its content.

So What's Driving the Party?

As the foregoing suggests, very few M&A deals create value and those that do generally require careful management and a very good understanding of what drives the value of the acquired company. Not many acquirers, to be honest, have the capability to acquire. So why do so many companies persist with M&A as a strategy?

As with many things in the marketplace, the answer is perverse incentives. The system in which CEOs operate is biased in two ways in favor of playing the M&A lottery. First, with the rise in stock-based compensation since the 1990s, the value of a successful acquisition bet is greatly enhanced for the CEO. If the acquisition gives the stock price a positive "pop," the personal benefit to the CEO is huge. Furthermore, compensation packages are strongly correlated with the size of the company, and an acquisition makes it bigger. Even failed acquisitions can be personally profitable. The Mattel–Learning Company and HP-Autonomy deals are among the most disastrous in recent memory, and they did cost CEOs Jill Barad and Léo Apotheker their jobs. But Barad left with a $40 million severance package, and Apotheker left with $25 million.

The second bias (at least in the United States) comes from an unlikely source: the Financial Accounting Standards Board. Before the dot-com bubble burst, in 2001, intangible assets were written off over a forty-year period. After the burst, assets valued at billions of dollars were seen to be worthless, so the FASB decided that in the future, a company's auditors would declare whether intangible assets were impaired and, if so, would force them to be written down immediately by the amount of the impairment.

The unintended consequence of this change was to make acquisitions more attractive because the acquiring company's earnings would no longer be suppressed every year by an automatic write-off. In the modern era of acquisitions, therefore, all a CEO has to do is convince the auditor that the acquired asset isn't impaired and that an acquisition will have no negative impact on earnings, even if it's made at an extraordinary price. Generally, this is fairly straightforward as long as the company's core business is doing well, and its market cap is higher than its book value.

• • •

Given the systematic bias in favor of deal-making, to which we can add the macho psychology and ego boost of the big deal or the vested interest of financial advisers, it's likely that we'll continue to witness more and more value-destroying deals in the coming years. But that should not necessarily put you off doing deals yourself. If you change your thinking about M&A, it can be a very successful way to grow. The secret is to stop thinking about acquisitions as if targets were jewels to be mined. Think of M&A rather as a meeting of minds, in which the acquirer helps the target to fully realize its value-creating potential by making new opportunities available, offering smarter management, and providing access to new and complementary capabilities.

This chapter is adapted from Roger L. Martin, "M&A: The One Thing You Need to Get Right," *Harvard Business Review*, June 2016.

Afterword

I hope that this book has got you thinking—or, more accurately, rethinking. You will probably have experienced the sting of these dominant models failing you—not all fourteen but probably more than a few. I hope I have convinced you that you should stop blaming yourself for having applied the model poorly. Chances are that it wasn't your fault—it was the model's fault.

I don't expect you to completely adopt the alternative model that I have presented in each chapter based on my argument. But I do hope that you give the alternative model a try. That is how you will move ahead and learn. You won't learn by continuing to reapply the flawed model and experience its ineffectiveness; you will simply reconfirm that it doesn't deliver. It's by trying models, observing the results, and then experimenting with a new model when the promised results don't materialize that you will embark on a positive learning journey.

And as you progress on that journey, keep in mind that you're the boss: *you own your models.* If you keep blaming yourself for the failure of the model that you are using yet keep on trying to use that model more effectively, then your model owns you. It is as if you have conferred it a monopoly on the use of your brain. If, instead, you hold your model accountable for producing the results that it promises and jettisoning it when it comes up short in repeated trials, then you own your models. If they don't perform for you, toss them out.

Of course, you should give the existing model a fair chance of working. Models don't become dominant for no reason. But I would encourage a healthy impatience. A model is a form of promise: if you use me, I will produce the following results for you. As with any product, if it fails conspicuously to fulfill its promise, you should not feel any obligation to keep buying it.

I am, however, realistic. I will go to my grave with some number of the models I propose not getting adopted more generally. Perhaps the one on which I'd give the longest odds is my approach to execution, described in chapter 10. My pessimism is based on two rather depressing recent conversations I have had around the idea—one with a scholar, among the world's leading handful of management scholars; the other with a practitioner, the head of training and development for a prominent Bay Area tech company. In both cases we were talking about the frequently quoted saying that "a mediocre idea well executed is superior to a great idea poorly executed," which both had used: the scholar in a tweet and the practitioner in a statement of company principles.

I asked each a fundamental question about the logic of their assertion: How would they know that an idea was "great" if it was "poorly executed"? You could well imagine how you would know if you had "a mediocre idea that was well executed." The results would be as expected and would be mediocre. And you can well imagine how you would know that something was poorly executed. The results would be disappointingly worse than expected. But how would you know whether the idea behind it was great or not when the only thing that is observable is that the idea failed to deliver?

The practitioner had no answer. That is, she had no ideas on how she would judge whether the idea in question was "great." When I asked her how she could support a principle of her company that "a mediocre idea well executed is superior to a great idea poorly executed" when she couldn't even define what a great idea is, she said that it was an important principle to ensure action orientation. Unfortunately, it didn't occur to her that the principle would guarantee an action orientation focused on mediocre ideas. Disappointingly, she showed zero interest in considering the viability or advisability of the model to which she dedicated herself.

The scholar, of course, had an answer. Scholars always have an answer. To him, the greatness of an idea should be judged by a panel of experts who opine on whether the idea is "novel" and "technically brilliant." However, in the business context, "well executed" means commercially successful. When I pointed out that there is no known correlation between expert opinion on novelty or technical brilliance and commercial success, he simply restated the proposition in a different way: "Creativity is the potential of an idea, and execution is the extent to which that potential is realized." Of course, there was no definition of potential or how it would be measured in his response. I gave up trying any further.

Clearly both the scholar and practitioner are owned by the model: "a mediocre idea well executed is superior to a great idea poorly executed." And of course, both work away assiduously on the problem of why the execution of great ideas is so poor and on improvements to "execution practices." I predict they will be working on that problem without progress for a long, long time.

My hope for you is that, unlike the scholar and practitioner, you will open your mind just a crack for each of the fourteen models. Imagine for a moment that a model the business world holds near and dear is, in fact, flawed and in response, experiment with a different model. If it doesn't work better, I fully endorse you going back to the dominant model. But the more you and others test the fourteen alternative models, the further the practice of management will advance. By observing the results of their use, you will be able to see things that I haven't seen and further advance the models, which will enhance the net effectiveness of management. And that is my purpose for writing this book.

Index

Acknowledgments

I have two expressions of gratitude that rank above the rest. I have flipped a coin on which to start with—heads, my editor, and tails, my coauthors. It was heads!

I owe a twelve-year debt of gratitude to my primary *Harvard Business Review* (HBR) editor, David Champion. He was assigned to an article I had submitted to HBR in 2009 (and was published in 2010). I had written eight HBR articles previously with a variety of editors, so I assumed that after this article, someone else would be the editor. But it was such an enjoyable and productive experience, I hoped that I was wrong. And I was. HBR kept assigning David to my submissions, and by 2021, we had published twenty together. Eleven of those twenty represent chapters in the book, and a new one in 2022, the twelfth. Plus, he helped me develop and edit the remaining two, one based on my 1993 HBR article and the other an entirely new piece.

David is a terrific editor and a great partner to work with. I generally send him too much prose containing too many ideas, and he helps figure out the most compelling ideas and the best way to present them. He makes me better, which is the best thing an editor can do for a writer.

In addition, the book was his idea. He saw a through line across my articles with him that I think is compelling. So, thank you, David.

Five of the chapters were originally written as HBR articles with coauthors, all of whom were fabulous contributors to the written product.

Two were coauthored with my longtime friend and collaborator, A.G. Lafley. Not surprisingly, given his well-known interests in both subjects, they are "Customers" (chapter 3) and "Strategy" (chapter 4). My relationship with A.G. goes back decades, and it is hard to entirely untangle from whose mind a given idea arose because it probably came from both of our heads.

Chapter 4 had two additional coauthors. The first is Jan Rivkin, who worked with me at Monitor Company and then left to pursue what has turned out to be a fabulously successful academic career at Harvard Business School. He was the inspiration for writing the article. He learned the strategy development process featured in the article from me while at Monitor and taught it to his HBS students to an enthusiastic reception. Based on the success in teaching it, he came to believe that it would make an excellent HBR article. His good friend, Nicolaj Siggelkow, a terrific Wharton strategy professor, also taught the material and became an integral part of the article-writing team. The foursome turned out to be an awesome team, and I am grateful to all three coauthors for their contributions to this chapter.

My coauthor for the original HBR article featured in "Choices," chapter 5, was Tony Golsby-Smith. I met Tony, an Australian who is the founder of Second Road, an innovation consulting firm in Sydney, through my work in design. During our work together, he convinced me that helping the business world understand Aristotle's thinking could contribute to better innovation outcomes. In due course, we decided to write an HBR article together. It took a very long time, the longest of all of my HBR articles, but was worth the effort.

My coauthor for the original HBR article featured in "Corporate Functions," chapter 8, is my longtime colleague and coauthor of *Creating Great Choices,* Jennifer Riel. Together we worked so often on helping functions do strategy that we thought the world needed its first article on why and how to do functional strategy. It was great to work with Jennifer on an article that lays the foundation for a subject as important as the strategy of functions in modern business.

Last but not least, my coauthor for the original HBR article featured in "Innovation," chapter 12, is my longtime collaborator on everything design, Tim Brown. We have worked on the intersection of design and strategy for many years, and this was one of the products of that collaboration.

So, thank you, thank you, A.G., Jan, Nicolaj, Tony, Jennifer, and Tim. Your collaborations have been instrumental to this book.

This is my eighth book with Harvard Business Review Press (HBR Press). I have a wonderful team there. Jeff Kehoe has been the acquiring editor for all eight of the books. HBR editor-in-chief and HBR Press publisher Adi Ignatius is always a wonderful supporter of my work at HBR Press and HBR. In addition, the team of Sally Ashworth, Julie Devoll, Stephani Finks, Erika Heilman, Felicia Sinusas, and Anne Starr has been terrific as always.

On this book, I am again working with the publicity team of Barbara Henricks and Jessica Krakoski of Cave Henricks, and it has, once again, been a great pleasure.

Finally, I want to thank my wife, Marie-Louise Skafte. My greatest period of writing and thinking productivity has been since 2013, the year I met Marie-Louise. I do not think that is a coincidence! Thanks, Marie-Louise, for being a great partner, supporter, and muse.

—Roger Martin
Fort Lauderdale, Florida

About the Author

ROGER L. MARTIN was named the world's number one management thinker in 2017 by Thinkers50, a biannual ranking of the most influential global business thinkers. He serves as a trusted strategy adviser to the CEOs of companies worldwide, including Procter & Gamble, Lego, and Ford.

Martin is a Professor of Strategic Management, Emeritus, at the University of Toronto's Rotman School of Management, where he served as dean from 1998 to 2013. In 2013 he was named global Dean of the Year by the leading business-school website, Poets & Quants.

Martin is the author of twelve books, including *Creating Great Choices*, written with Jennifer Riel; *Getting Beyond Better*, written with Sally Osberg; and *Playing to Win*, written with A.G. Lafley, which won the Thinkers50 Best Book Award for 2013. In addition, he has written thirty articles for *Harvard Business Review*.

Martin received his AB from Harvard College, with a concentration in economics, in 1979 and his MBA from Harvard Business School in 1981. He lives in South Florida with his wife, Marie-Louise Skafte.